Crock Pot

Cookbook for Beginners 2023

1000+ Healthy and Delicious Crockpot Recipes With Only 5
Ingredients or Less For all Beginners and Advanced Users

Emma Roberts

1 Crock Pot
Cookbook

CONTENTS

Chapter 5 Poultry Recipes 43

Chapter 11 Dessert Recipes 112

APPENDIX : Recipes Index 126

Introduction

Hi,Thank you for choosing this cookbook!In this book, we will explore 1000 quick,easy and delicious dishes you can cook with your Crock Pot.And you will explore a wide range of dishes (breakfasts, stews, desserts, and more),and they all use Only 5 healthy ingredients in the entire cooking process. All the recipes ate required a maximum Only five components. Each recipe contains the preparation time, nutritional information, cooking instructions, and ingredients that are necessary to prepare the dishes. Once you try these delicious dishes with this cookbook, you and your Crock Pot are sure to become inseparable.

My name is Emma Roberts. I am a cookbook author and a former chief who had worked in celebrated restaurant in los Angeles for more than 10 years .Now I am full time cookbook author.

As a huge fan of simple cooking, I have created numerous recipes over the years that have one major theme in mind: They're so easy that anyone can make them. I love food that is simple and straightforward but also full of flavor. Few years I had my Crock Pot as gift from my friend few months.One day as I began to use it ,I quickly fell in love with it .It's simplicity and multi-functional.Now it has become my essential kitchen appliance which I cook with it everyday ,almost every meal.

This book has been carefully written to meet the needs of everyone who likes cooking , would like to save money, would like to taste flavorful dish which retain most of the nutrition ,who like save the trouble to prepare food. They are chosen from loads of 5-ingredient, Crock Pot recipes that take 15-minutes or less to prepare .All the recipes are one-pot meals You won't need sides due to this slow cooker recipes are complete, delicious, and satisfying meals all on their own. You will even find out a lot of tricks and hack to make Crock Pot recipes more tasty and reduce more cooking and preparing time .I guarantee that you'll get the hang of using Crock Pot. And with every meal you make, you'll grow more comfortable.

Read on and learn more!

Chapter 1 Getting Started with Your Crock Pot

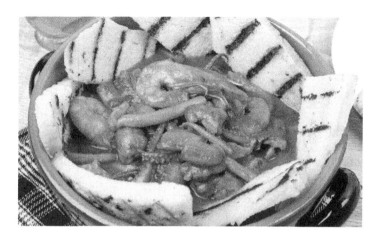

What is a Crock Pot?

Crock pot, technically this device is called an electric heating oven (no matter the brand) and features a ceramic or porcelain pot that fits snugly into the crock with a glass lid to trap the heat and moisture inside.

The device has two heat settings, high (typically 300°F) and low (200°F), with most models now coming with a "Keep Warm" setting. It cooks food slowly at a low temperature, with the heat surrounding the food and bringing it up to a safe temperature quickly.

Direct heat from the crock, a lengthy cooking period, and steam created in the tightly covered container all combine to destroy any bacteria, which makes this method of cooking a safe process.

How to use Crock Pot?

·Turn it on: Ask anyone who uses their Crock Pot regularly and they will tell you a time when they forgot to plug it in or turn it on. It's almost a right of passage. Always make sure to check that you turned it on before you walk away.

·Keep the lid closed: Leave your Crock Pot alone! This is one of the benefits of cooking in a Crock Pot is that you just throw everything in and leave it to cook. Every time you lift the lid it will add 15-20 minutes of cook time because you release the heat that was inside it.

·Don't add too much liquid: Slow Cookers don't allow for very much evaporation with their tight-fitting so you don't want to add too much liquid.

·Choose the right cut of meat– The best cuts of meat to use in a slow cooker are tough meats with a little more fat that lend themself to cooking for longer times like chicken thighs, beef roasts, and pork roasts. If you are cooking leaner meat like chicken breasts and pork tenderloin just make sure to cook it for a shorter time.

How to clean Crock Pot?

1. Remove Excess Residues

Rinse the crock-pot to remove as much food and residues from the inner container then make a paste. Add Powerizer to a dish brush and apply Powerizer in a paste to the stained areas, which are usually near the top at the waterline or the bottom.

2. Prepare A Soak

For tougher stains, a soak may be necessary. Fill the crock-pot with enough water to cover the stained areas.

3. Add Powerizer

Next, Sprinkle in one (1) scoop of Powerizer into the pot and set the heat to it's lowest temperature. Our powerful plant-based enzymes are why one small scoop is so effective at cleaning everything dirty. These natural enzymes activate in water to quickly dissolve protein and starch found in stains. Meanwhile, a hard water softener allows the detergent to dissolve the white mineral stains.

4. Rest Your Feet, Let It Soak

Cover the pot to trap in steam and set the temperature to the lowest setting. Allow the detergent to cook as long as needed; however, be sure not to allow the water to evaporate completely.

5. Wipe Or Scrub Away Food Debris

Usually, slow cooking the detergent for an hour is all that is needed. However, for tough stains, more time may be necessary. The oxidizing agent (sodium percarbonate) found in Powerizer; remains active for up to 8 hours. Set a timer to check the crock-pot every couple of hours to determine if the stains have dissolved. Scrub the stains when necessary using a copper or nylon hand dish scrubber.

6. Rinse And Polish To Remove Residues.

Rinse the detergent with plain water to remove any residues and detergent—Polish and dry the inner pot and outer container using a damp microfiber cloth.

Maintenance tip for your Crock Pot

ALWAYS turn your unit off, unplug it from the electrical outlet, and allow it to cool before cleaning. Dishwasher safe parts can be washed in the dishwasher or with hot, soapy water. Do not use abrasive cleaning compounds or scouring pads. A cloth, sponge, or rubber spatula will usually remove residue. To remove water spots and other stains, use a non-abrasive cleaner or vinegar. As with any fine ceramic, the stoneware and lid will not withstand sudden temperature changes. Do not wash the stoneware or lid with cold water when they are hot.

Measurement Conversions

BASIC KITCHEN CONVERSIONS & EQUIVALENTS

DRY MEASUREMENTS CONVERSION CHART

3 TEASPOONS = 1 TABLESPOON = 1/16 CUP

6 TEASPOONS = 2 TABLESPOONS = 1/8 CUP

12 TEASPOONS = 4 TABLESPOONS = 1/4 CUP

24 TEASPOONS = 8 TABLESPOONS = 1/2 CUP

36 TEASPOONS = 12 TABLESPOONS = 3/4 CUP

48 TEASPOONS = 16 TABLESPOONS = 1 CUP

METRIC TO US COOKING CONVERSIONS

OVEN TEMPERATURES

120 °C = 250 °F

160 °C = 320 °F

180° C = 350 °F

205 °C = 400 °F

220 °C = 425 °F

LIQUID MEASUREMENTS CONVERSION CHART

8 FLUID OUNCES = 1 CUP = 1/2 PINT = 1/4 QUART

16 FLUID OUNCES = 2 CUPS = 1 PINT = 1/2 QUART

32 FLUID OUNCES = 4 CUPS = 2 PINTS = 1 QUART = 1/4 GALLON

128 FLUID OUNCES = 16 CUPS = 8 PINTS = 4 QUARTS = 1 GALLON

BAKING IN GRAMS

1 CUP FLOUR = 140 GRAMS

1 CUP SUGAR = 150 GRAMS

1 CUP POWDERED SUGAR = 160 GRAMS

1 CUP HEAVY CREAM = 235 GRAMS

VOLUME

1 MILLILITER = 1/5 TEASPOON

5 ML = 1 TEASPOON

15 ML = 1 TABLESPOON

240 ML = 1 CUP OR 8 FLUID OUNCES

1 LITER = 34 FL. OUNCES

WEIGHT

1 GRAM = .035 OUNCES

100 GRAMS = 3.5 OUNCES

500 GRAMS = 1.1 POUNDS

1 KILOGRAM = 35 OUNCES

US TO METRIC COOKING CONVERSIONS

1/5 TSP = 1 ML

1 TSP = 5 ML

1 TBSP = 15 ML

1 FL OUNCE = 30 ML

1 CUP = 237 ML

1 PINT (2 CUPS) = 473 ML

1 QUART (4 CUPS) = .95 LITER

1 GALLON (16 CUPS) = 3.8 LITERS

1 OZ = 28 GRAMS

1 POUND = 454 GRAMS

BUTTER

1 CUP BUTTER = 2 STICKS = 8 OUNCES = 230 GRAMS = 8 TABLESPOONS

WHAT DOES 1 CUP EQUAL

1 CUP = 8 FLUID OUNCES

1 CUP = 16 TABLESPOONS

1 CUP = 48 TEASPOONS

1 CUP = 1/2 PINT

1 CUP = 1/4 QUART

1 CUP = 1/16 GALLON

1 CUP = 240 ML

BAKING PAN CONVERSIONS

1 CUP ALL-PURPOSE FLOUR = 4.5 OZ

1 CUP ROLLED OATS = 3 OZ 1 LARGE EGG = 1.7 OZ

1 CUP BUTTER = 8 OZ 1 CUP MILK = 8 OZ

1 CUP HEAVY CREAM = 8.4 OZ

1 CUP GRANULATED SUGAR = 7.1 OZ

1 CUP PACKED BROWN SUGAR = 7.75 OZ

1 CUP VEGETABLE OIL = 7.7 OZ

1 CUP UNSIFTED POWDERED SUGAR = 4.4 OZ

BAKING PAN CONVERSIONS

9-INCH ROUND CAKE PAN = 12 CUPS

10-INCH TUBE PAN =16 CUPS

11-INCH BUNDT PAN = 12 CUPS

9-INCH SPRINGFORM PAN = 10 CUPS

9 X 5 INCH LOAF PAN = 8 CUPS

9-INCH SQUARE PAN = 8 CUPS

Chapter 2 Breakfast Recipes

Chapter 2 Breakfast Recipes

Shredded Chicken Muffins

Servings:4 | Cooking Time: 2.5 Hours

Ingredients:
- 6 oz chicken fillet, boiled
- 4 eggs, beaten
- 1 teaspoon salt
- 1 teaspoon ground black pepper
- 1 teaspoon olive oil

Directions:
1. Shred the chicken fillet with the help of the fork and mix with eggs, salt, and ground black pepper.
2. Then brush the muffin molds with olive oil and transfer the shredded chicken mixture inside.
3. Put the muffins in the Crock Pot.
4. Close the lid and cook them on High for 2.5 hours.

Nutrition Info:
- Per Serving: 155 calories, 17.9g protein, 0.7g carbohydrates, 8.7g fat, 0.1g fiber, 202mg cholesterol, 680mg sodium, 169mg potassium

Bacon Eggs

Servings:2 | Cooking Time: 2 Hours

Ingredients:
- 2 bacon slices
- 2 eggs, hard-boiled, peeled
- ¼ teaspoon ground black pepper
- 1 teaspoon olive oil
- ½ teaspoon dried thyme

Directions:
1. Sprinkle the bacon with ground black pepper and dried thyme.
2. Then wrap the eggs in the bacon and sprinkle with olive oil.
3. Put the eggs in the Crock Pot and cook on High for 2 hours.

Nutrition Info:
- Per Serving: 187 calories, 12.6g protein, 0.9g carbohydrates, 14.7g fat, 0.2g fiber, 185mg cholesterol, 501mg sodium, 172mg potassium.

Broccoli Egg Casserole

Servings:5 | Cooking Time: 3 Hours

Ingredients:
- 4 eggs, beaten
- ½ cup full-fat milk
- 3 tablespoons grass-fed butter, melted
- 1 ½ cup broccoli florets, chopped
- Salt and pepper to taste

Directions:
1. Beat the eggs and milk in a mixing bowl.
2. Grease the bottom of the CrockPot with melted butter.
3. Add in the broccoli florets in the CrockPot and pour the egg mixture.
4. Season with salt and pepper to taste.
5. Close the lid and cook on high for 2 hours or on low for 3 hours.

Nutrition Info:
- Calories per serving: 217; Carbohydrates:4.6 g; Protein: 11.6g; Fat: 16.5g; Sugar: 0.7g; Sodium: 674mg; Fiber: 2.3g

Squash Butter

Servings:4 | Cooking Time: 2 Hours

Ingredients:
- 1 cup butternut squash puree
- 1 teaspoon allspices
- 4 tablespoons applesauce
- 2 tablespoons butter
- 1 teaspoon cornflour

Directions:
1. Put all ingredients in the Crock Pot and mix until homogenous.
2. Then close the lid and cook the butter on High for 2 hours.
3. Transfer the cooked squash butter in the plastic vessel and cool it well.

Nutrition Info:
- Per Serving: 78 calories, 0.2g protein, 6.3g carbohydrates, 5.8g fat, 0.8g fiber, 15mg cholesterol, 44mg sodium, 20mg potassium

Bacon Potatoes

Servings:4 | Cooking Time: 5 Hours

Ingredients:
- 4 russet potatoes
- 1 teaspoon dried thyme
- 4 teaspoons olive oil
- 4 bacon slices

Directions:
1. Cut the potatoes into halves and sprinkle with dried thyme and olive oil.
2. After this, cut every bacon slice into halves.
3. Put the potatoes in the Crock Pot bowl and top with bacon slices.
4. Close the lid and cook them for 5 hours on High.

Nutrition Info:
- Per Serving: 290 calories, 10.6g protein, 33.9g carbohydrates, 12.8g fat, 5.2g fiber, 21mg cholesterol, 452mg sodium, 976mg potassium.

Coconut Oatmeal

Servings:6 | Cooking Time: 5 Hours

Ingredients:
- 2 cups oatmeal
- 2 cups of coconut milk
- 1 cup of water
- 2 tablespoons coconut shred
- 1 tablespoon maple syrup

Directions:
1. Put all ingredients in the Crock Pot and carefully mix.
2. Then close the lid and cook the oatmeal on low for 5 hours.

Nutrition Info:
- Per Serving: 313 calories, 5.4g protein, 25.8g carbohydrates, 22.5g fat, 4.8g fiber, 0mg cholesterol, 16mg sodium, 316mg potassium

Basil Sausages

Servings:5 | Cooking Time: 4 Hours

Ingredients:
- 1-pound Italian sausages, chopped
- 1 teaspoon dried basil
- 1 tablespoon olive oil
- 1 teaspoon ground coriander
- ¼ cup of water

Directions:
1. Sprinkle the chopped sausages with ground coriander and dried basil and transfer in the Crock Pot.
2. Add olive oil and water.
3. Close the lid and cook the sausages on high for 4 hours.

Nutrition Info:
- Per Serving: 338 calories, 12.9g protein, 0.6g carbohydrates, 31.2g fat, 0g fiber, 69mg cholesterol, 664mg sodium, 231mg potassium.

Caramel Pecan Sticky Buns

Servings: 4 | Cooking Time: 2 Hours 40 Minutes

Ingredients:
- ¾ cup packed brown sugar
- 15 ounces refrigerated biscuits
- 1 teaspoon ground cinnamon
- 6 tablespoons melted butter
- ¼ cup pecans, finely chopped

Directions:
1. Mix together brown sugar, cinnamon and chopped nuts in a bowl.
2. Dip refrigerator biscuits in melted butter to coat, then in the brown sugar mixture.
3. Grease a crockpot and layer the biscuits in the crock pot.
4. Top with the remaining brown sugar mixture and cover the lid.
5. Cook on HIGH for about 2 hours and dish out to serve.

Nutrition Info:
- Calories: 583 Fat: 23.5g Carbohydrates: 86.2g

Chorizo Eggs

Servings:4 | Cooking Time: 1.5 Hours

Ingredients:
- 5 oz chorizo, sliced
- 4 eggs, beaten
- 2 oz Parmesan, grated
- 1 teaspoon butter, softened

Directions:
1. Grease the Crock Pot bottom with butter.
2. Add chorizo and cook them on high for 30 minutes.
3. Then flip the sliced chorizo and add eggs and Par-

13 Crock Pot Cookbook

mesan.

4. Close the lid and cook the meal on High for 1 hour more.

Nutrition Info:
- Per Serving: 278 calories, 18.6g protein, 1.5g carbohydrates, 21.9g fat, 0g fiber, 208mg cholesterol, 638mg sodium, 200mg potassium

Broccoli Omelet

Servings:4 | Cooking Time: 2 Hours

Ingredients:
- 5 eggs, beaten
- 1 tablespoon cream cheese
- 3 oz broccoli, chopped
- 1 tomato, chopped
- 1 teaspoon avocado oil

Directions:
1. Mix eggs with cream cheese and transfer in the Crock Pot.
2. Add avocado oil, broccoli, and tomato.
3. Close the lid and cook the omelet on High for 2 hours.

Nutrition Info:
- Per Serving: 99 calories, 7.9g protein, 2.6g carbohydrates, 6.6g fat, 0.8g fiber, 207mg cholesterol, 92mg sodium, 184mg potassium.

Orange Pudding

Servings:4 | Cooking Time: 4 Hours

Ingredients:
- 1 cup carrot, grated
- 2 cups of milk
- 1 tablespoon cornstarch
- 1 teaspoon vanilla extract
- ½ teaspoon ground nutmeg

Directions:
1. Put the carrot in the Crock Pot.
2. Add milk, vanilla extract, and ground nutmeg.
3. Then add cornstarch and stir the ingredients until cornstarch is dissolved.
4. Cook the pudding on low for 4 hours.

Nutrition Info:
- Per Serving: 84 calories, 4.3g protein, 10.8g carbohydrates, 2.6g fat, 0.8g fiber, 10mg cholesterol, 77mg sodium, 161mg potassium.

Egg Scramble

Servings:4 | Cooking Time: 2.5 Hours

Ingredients:
- 4 eggs, beaten
- 1 tablespoon butter, melted
- 2 oz Cheddar cheese, shredded
- ¼ teaspoon cayenne pepper
- 1 teaspoon ground paprika

Directions:
1. Mix eggs with butter, cheese, cayenne pepper, and ground paprika.
2. Then pour the mixture in the Crock Pot and close the lid.
3. Cook it on high for 2 hours.
4. Then open the lid and scramble the eggs.
5. Close the lid and cook the meal on high for 30 minutes.

Nutrition Info:
- Per Serving: 147 calories, 9.2g protein, 0.9g carbohydrates, 12g fat, 0.2g fiber, 186mg cholesterol, 170mg sodium, 88mg potassium.

Eggs With Brussel Sprouts

Servings:4 | Cooking Time: 6 Hours

Ingredients:
- 1 cup Brussel sprouts, halved
- ½ cup Mozzarella, shredded
- 5 eggs, beaten
- 1 teaspoon chili powder
- 1 teaspoon olive oil

Directions:
1. Pour olive oil in the Crock Pot.
2. Then add the layer of the Brussel sprouts.
3. Sprinkle the vegetables with chili powder and eggs.
4. Then add mozzarella and close the lid.
5. Cook the meal on Low for 6 hours.

Nutrition Info:
- Per Serving: 110 calories, 8.8g protein, 2.9g carbohydrates, 7.5g fat, 1.1g fiber, 206mg cholesterol, 110mg sodium, 172mg potassium

Apricot Oatmeal

Servings:4 | Cooking Time: 4 Hours

Ingredients:
- 1 ½ cup oatmeal
- 1 cup of water
- 3 cups of milk
- 1 cup apricots, pitted, sliced
- 1 teaspoon butter

Directions:
1. Put oatmeal in the Crock Pot.
2. Add water, milk, and butter.
3. Close the lid and cook the mixture on high for 1 hour.
4. Then add apricots, carefully mix the oatmeal and close the lid.
5. Cook the meal on Low for 3 hours.

Nutrition Info:
- Per Serving: 235 calories, 10.5g protein, 34g carbohydrates, 7g fat, 3.9g fiber, 18mg cholesterol, 97mg sodium, 317mg potassium

Raspberry Chia Pudding

Servings:2 | Cooking Time: 2 Hours

Ingredients:
- 4 tablespoons chia seeds
- 1 cup of coconut milk
- 2 teaspoons raspberries

Directions:
1. Put chia seeds and coconut milk in the Crock Pot and cook it for 2 hours on Low.
2. Then transfer the cooked chia pudding in the glasses and top with raspberries.

Nutrition Info:
- Per Serving: 423 calories, 7.7g protein, 19.6g carbohydrates, 37.9g fat, 13.1g fiber, 0mg cholesterol, 23mg sodium, 442mg potassium.

Creamy Bacon Millet

Servings: 6 | Cooking Time: 4 Hrs 10 Minutes

Ingredients:
- 3 cup millet
- 6 cup chicken stock
- 1 tsp salt
- 4 tbsp heavy cream

- 5 oz. bacon, chopped

Directions:
1. Add millet and chicken stock to the Crock Pot.
2. Stir in chopped bacon and salt.
3. Put the cooker's lid on and set the cooking time to 4 hours on High settings.
4. Stir in cream and again cover the lid of the Crock Pot.
5. Cook for 10 minutes on High setting.
6. Serve.

Nutrition Info:
- Per Serving: Calories 572, Total Fat 17.8g, Fiber 9g, Total Carbs 83.09g, Protein 20g

Chia Oatmeal

Servings: 2 | Cooking Time: 8 Hours

Ingredients:
- 2 cups almond milk
- 1 cup steel cut oats
- 2 tablespoons butter, soft
- ½ teaspoon almond extract
- 2 tablespoons chia seeds

Directions:
1. In your Crock Pot, mix the oats with the chia seeds and the other ingredients, toss, put the lid on and cook on Low for 8 hours.
2. Stir the oatmeal one more time, divide into 2 bowls and serve.

Nutrition Info:
- calories 812, fat 71.4, fiber 9.4, carbs 41.1, protein 11

Carrot Pudding

Servings:4 | Cooking Time: 5 Hours

Ingredients:
- 3 cups carrot, shredded
- 1 tablespoon potato starch
- 3 tablespoons maple syrup
- 1 teaspoon ground cinnamon
- 4 cups of milk

Directions:
1. Mix potato starch with milk and pour the liquid in the Crock Pot.
2. Add ground cinnamon, maple syrup, and carrot.
3. Close the lid and cook the pudding on Low for 5

hours.

Nutrition Info:
- Per Serving: 206 calories, 8.7g protein, 33.1g carbohydrates, 5g fat, 2.3g fiber, 20mg cholesterol, 173mg sodium, 437mg potassium

French Breakfast Pudding

Servings: 4 | Cooking Time: 1 Hour And 30 Minutes

Ingredients:
- 3 egg yolks
- 6 ounces double cream
- 1 teaspoon vanilla extract
- 2 tablespoons caster sugar

Directions:
1. In a bowl, mix the egg yolks with sugar and whisk well.
2. Add cream and vanilla extract, whisk well, pour into your 4 ramekins, place them in your Crock Pot, add some water to the Crock Pot, cover and cook on High for 1 hour and 30 minutes.
3. Leave aside to cool down and serve.

Nutrition Info:
- calories 261, fat 5, fiber 6, carbs 15, protein 2

Salami Eggs

Servings:4 | Cooking Time: 2.5 Hours

Ingredients:
- 4 oz salami, sliced
- 4 eggs
- 1 teaspoon butter, melted
- 1 tablespoon chives, chopped

Directions:
1. Pour the melted butter in the Crock Pot.
2. Crack the eggs inside.
3. Then top the eggs with salami and chives.
4. Close the lid and cook them on High for 2.5 hours.

Nutrition Info:
- Per Serving: 146 calories, 9.1g protein, 0.9g carbohydrates, 11.6g fat, 0g fiber, 186mg cholesterol, 392mg sodium, 115mg potassium

Peach, Vanilla And Oats Mix

Servings: 2 | Cooking Time: 8 Hours

Ingredients:
- ½ cup steel cut oats
- 2 cups almond milk
- ½ cup peaches, pitted and roughly chopped
- ½ teaspoon vanilla extract
- 1 teaspoon cinnamon powder

Directions:
1. In your Crock Pot, mix the oats with the almond milk, peaches and the other ingredients, toss, put the lid on and cook on Low for 8 hours.
2. Divide into bowls and serve for breakfast right away.

Nutrition Info:
- calories 261, fat 5, fiber 8, carbs 18, protein 6

Raspberry Chia Porridge

Servings:4 | Cooking Time: 4 Hours

Ingredients:
- 1 cup raspberry
- 3 tablespoons maple syrup
- 1 cup chia seeds
- 4 cups of milk

Directions:
1. Put chia seeds and milk in the Crock Pot and cook the mixture on low for 4 hours.
2. Meanwhile, mix raspberries and maple syrup in the blender and blend the mixture until smooth.
3. When the chia porridge is cooked, transfer it in the serving bowls and top with blended raspberry mixture.

Nutrition Info:
- Per Serving: 315 calories, 13.1g protein, 37.7g carbohydrates, 13.9g fat, 11.7g fiber, 20mg cholesterol, 121mg sodium, 332mg potassium

Smoked Salmon Omelet

Servings:4 | Cooking Time: 2 Hours

Ingredients:
- 4 oz smoked salmon, sliced
- 5 eggs, beaten
- 1 teaspoon ground coriander
- 1 teaspoon butter, melted

Directions:

1. Brush the Crock Pot bottom with melted butter.
2. Then mix eggs with ground coriander and pour the liquid in the Crock Pot.
3. Add smoked salmon and close the lid.
4. Cook the omelet on High for 2 hours.

Nutrition Info:
- Per Serving: 120 calories, 12.1g protein, 0.4g carbohydrates, 7.7g fat, 0g fiber, 214mg cholesterol, 651mg sodium, 124mg potassium

Breakfast Monkey Bread

Servings:6 | Cooking Time: 6 Hours

Ingredients:
- 10 oz biscuit rolls
- 1 tablespoon ground cardamom
- 1 tablespoon sugar
- 2 tablespoons coconut oil
- 1 egg, beaten

Directions:
1. Chop the biscuit roll roughly.
2. Mix sugar with ground cardamom.
3. Melt the coconut oil.
4. Put the ½ part of chopped biscuit rolls in the Crock Pot in one layer and sprinkle with melted coconut oil and ½ part of all ground cinnamon mixture.
5. Then top it with remaining biscuit roll chops and sprinkle with cardamom mixture and coconut oil.
6. Then brush the bread with a beaten egg and close the lid.
7. Cook the meal on High for 6 hours.
8. Cook the cooked bread well.

Nutrition Info:
- Per Serving: 178 calories, 6.1g protein, 26.4g carbohydrates, 7g fat, 2g fiber, 27mg cholesterol, 238mg sodium, 21mg potassium.

Kale Cups

Servings:4 | Cooking Time: 2.5 Hours

Ingredients:
- 1 cup kale, chopped
- 4 eggs, beaten
- 1 teaspoon olive oil
- 1 teaspoon chili powder
- ½ cup Cheddar cheese, shredded

Directions:

1. Mix kale with eggs, olive oil, and chili powder.
2. Transfer the mixture in the ramekins and top with Cheddar cheese.
3. Place the ramekins in the Crock Pot.
4. Close the lid and cook the meal on high for 2.5 hours.

Nutrition Info:
- Per Serving: 140 calories, 9.6g protein, 2.6g carbohydrates, 10.3g fat, 0.5g fiber, 179mg cholesterol, 163mg sodium, 168mg potassium

Sweet Quinoa

Servings:4 | Cooking Time: 3 Hours

Ingredients:
- 1 cup quinoa
- ¼ cup dates, chopped
- 3 cups of water
- 1 apricot, chopped
- ½ teaspoon ground nutmeg

Directions:
1. Put quinoa, dates, and apricot in the Crock Pot.
2. Add ground nutmeg and mix the mixture.
3. Cook it on high for 3 hours.

Nutrition Info:
- Per Serving: 194 calories, 6.4g protein, 36.7g carbohydrates, 2.8g fat, 4.1g fiber, 0mg cholesterol, 8g sodium, 338mg potassium.

Leek Bake

Servings:3 | Cooking Time: 8 Hours

Ingredients:
- 2 cups leek, chopped
- 3 oz Cheddar cheese, shredded
- ¼ cup ground chicken
- 1 teaspoon dried thyme
- ½ cup chicken stock

Directions:
1. Pour the chicken stock in the Crock Pot.
2. Put the leek in the chicken stock and sprinkle it with dried thyme and ground chicken.
3. Then top the chicken with Cheddar cheese and close the lid.
4. Cook the leek bake on low for 8 hours.

Nutrition Info:
- Per Serving: 175 calories, 11.5g protein, 9.1g car-

bohydrates, 10.6g fat, 1.2g fiber, 40mg cholesterol, 325mg sodium, 168mg potassium.

Milk Pudding

Servings:2 | Cooking Time: 7 Hours

Ingredients:
- 1 cup milk
- 3 eggs, beaten
- 2 tablespoons cornstarch
- 1 teaspoon vanilla extract
- 1 tablespoon white sugar

Directions:
1. Mix milk with eggs and cornstarch.
2. Whisk the mixture until smooth and add vanilla extract and white sugar.
3. Pour the liquid in the Crock Pot and close the lid.
4. Cook it on Low for 7 hours.

Nutrition Info:
- Per Serving: 214 calories, 12.3g protein, 20.1g carbohydrates, 9.1g fat, 9.7g fiber, 0.1mg cholesterol, 151mg sodium, 162mg potassium.

Mocha Latte Quinoa Mix

Servings: 4 | Cooking Time: 6 Hours

Ingredients:
- 1 cup hot coffee
- 1 cup quinoa
- 1 cup coconut water
- ¼ cup chocolate chips
- ½ cup coconut cream

Directions:
1. In your Crock Pot, mix quinoa with coffee, coconut water and chocolate chips, cover and cook on Low for 6 hours.
2. Stir, divide into bowls, spread coconut cream all over and serve for breakfast.

Nutrition Info:
- calories 251, fat 4, fiber 7, carbs 15, protein 4

Raisins And Rice Pudding

Servings:4 | Cooking Time: 6 Hours

Ingredients:
- 1 cup long-grain rice
- 2.5 cups organic almond milk
- 2 tablespoons cornstarch
- 1 teaspoon vanilla extract
- 2 tablespoons raisins, chopped

Directions:
1. Put all ingredients in the Crock Pot and carefully mix.
2. Then close the lid and cook the pudding for 6 hours on Low.

Nutrition Info:
- Per Serving: 238 calories, 4.1g protein, 49.4g carbohydrates, 1.9g fat, 0.8g fiber, 0mg cholesterol, 91mg sodium, 89mg potassium

Breakfast Meat Rolls

Servings:12 | Cooking Time: 4.5 Hours

Ingredients:
- 1-pound puff pastry
- 1 cup ground pork
- 1 tablespoon garlic, diced
- 1 egg, beaten
- 1 tablespoon sesame oil

Directions:
1. Roll up the puff pastry.
2. Then mix ground pork with garlic and egg.
3. Then spread the puff pastry with ground meat mixture and roll.
4. Cut the puff pastry rolls on small rolls.
5. Then sprinkle the rolls with sesame oil.
6. Arrange the meat rolls in the Crock Pot and close the lid.
7. Cook breakfast on High for 4.5 hours.

Nutrition Info:
- Per Serving: 244 calories, 4.9g protein, 17.3g carbohydrates, 17.2g fat, 0.6g fiber, 20mg cholesterol, 106mg sodium, 31mg potassium.

Seafood Eggs

Servings:4 | Cooking Time: 2.5 Hours

Ingredients:
- 4 eggs, beaten
- 2 tablespoons cream cheese
- 1 teaspoon Italian seasonings
- 6 oz shrimps, peeled
- 1 teaspoon olive oil

Directions:
1. Mix cream cheese with eggs.
2. Add Italian seasonings and shrimps.
3. Then brush the ramekins with olive oil and pour the egg mixture inside.
4. Transfer the ramekins in the Crock Pot.
5. Cook the eggs on High for 2.5 hours.

Nutrition Info:
- Per Serving: 144 calories, 15.6g protein, 1.3g carbohydrates, 8.4g fat, 0g fiber, 260mg cholesterol, 181mg sodium, 138mg potassium

Peach Puree

Servings:2 | Cooking Time: 7 Hours

Ingredients:
- 2 cups peaches, chopped
- 1 tablespoon sugar
- 1 teaspoon ground cinnamon
- ¼ cup of water

Directions:
1. Put all ingredients in the Crock Pot.
2. Close the lid and cook them on low for 7 hours.
3. Then make the puree with the help of the immersion blender.
4. Store the puree in the fridge for up to 1 day.

Nutrition Info:
- Per Serving: 84 calories, 1.5g protein, 20.9g carbohydrates, 0.4g fat, 2.9g fiber, 0mg cholesterol, 1mg sodium, 290mg potassium

Salmon Frittata

Servings: 3 | Cooking Time: 3 Hours And 40 Minutes

Ingredients:
- 4 eggs, whisked
- ½ teaspoon olive oil
- 2 tablespoons green onions, chopped
- Salt and black pepper to the taste
- 4 ounces smoked salmon, chopped

Directions:
1. Drizzle the oil in your Crock Pot, add eggs, salt and pepper, whisk, cover and cook on Low for 3 hours.
2. Add salmon and green onions, toss a bit, cover, cook on Low for 40 minutes more and divide between plates.
3. Serve right away for breakfast.

Nutrition Info:
- calories 220, fat 10, fiber 2, carbs 15, protein 7

Peach Oats

Servings:3 | Cooking Time: 7 Hours

Ingredients:
- ½ cup steel cut oats
- 1 cup milk
- ½ cup peaches, pitted, chopped
- 1 teaspoon ground cardamom

Directions:
1. Mix steel-cut oats with milk and pour the mixture in the Crock Pot.
2. Add ground cardamom and peaches. Stir the ingredients gently and close the lid.
3. Cook the meal on low for 7 hours.

Nutrition Info:
- Per Serving: 159 calories, 7g protein, 24.8g carbohydrates, 3.8g fat, 3.2g fiber, 7mg cholesterol, 38mg sodium, 200mg potassium

Baby Carrots In Syrup

Servings:5 | Cooking Time: 7 Hours

Ingredients:
- 3 cups baby carrots
- 1 cup apple juice
- 2 tablespoons brown sugar
- 1 teaspoon vanilla extract

Directions:

1. Mix apple juice, brown sugar, and vanilla extract.
2. Pour the liquid in the Crock Pot.
3. Add baby carrots and close the lid.
4. Cook the meal on Low for 7 hours.

Nutrition Info:
- Per Serving: 81 calories, 0g protein, 18.8g carbohydrates, 0.1g fat, 3.7g fiber, 0mg cholesterol, 363mg sodium, 56mg potassium.

Cream Grits

Servings:2 | Cooking Time: 5 Hours

Ingredients:
- ½ cup grits
- ½ cup heavy cream
- 1 cup of water
- 1 tablespoon cream cheese

Directions:
1. Put grits, heavy cream, and water in the Crock Pot.
2. Cook the meal on LOW for 5 hours.
3. When the grits are cooked, add cream cheese and stir carefully.
4. Transfer the meal in the serving bowls.

Nutrition Info:
- Per Serving: 151 calories, 1.6g protein, 6.9g carbohydrates, 13.2g fat, 1g fiber, 47mg cholesterol, 116mg sodium, 33mg potassium.

Chocolate Oatmeal

Servings:5 | Cooking Time: 4 Hours

Ingredients:
- 1 oz dark chocolate, chopped
- 1 teaspoon vanilla extract
- 2 cups of coconut milk
- 2 cup oatmeal
- ½ teaspoon ground cardamom

Directions:
1. Put all ingredients in the Crock Pot and stir carefully with the help of the spoon.
2. Close the lid and cook the meal for 4 hours on Low.

Nutrition Info:
- Per Serving: 386 calories, 7.1g protein, 32.5g carbohydrates, 27.2g fat, 6.1g fiber,1mg cholesterol, 19mg sodium, 374mg potassium.

Honey Pumpkin

Servings:4 | Cooking Time: 7 Hours

Ingredients:
- 2 tablespoons honey
- 1 tablespoon ground cinnamon
- 1 tablespoon ground cardamom
- 1-pound pumpkin, cubed
- ¼ cup of water

Directions:
1. Put pumpkin in the Crock Pot.
2. Add honey, ground cinnamon, cardamom, and water. Mix the ingredients and close the lid.
3. Cook the pumpkin on Low for 7 hours.

Nutrition Info:
- Per Serving: 79 calories, 1.5g protein, 20.2g carbohydrates, 0.4g fat, 4.6g fiber, 0mg cholesterol, 7mg sodium, 263mg potassium.

Olive Eggs

Servings:4 | Cooking Time: 2 Hours

Ingredients:
- 10 kalamata olives, sliced
- 8 eggs, beaten
- 1 teaspoon cayenne pepper
- 1 tablespoon butter

Directions:
1. Grease the Crock Pot bottom with butter.
2. Then add beaten eggs and cayenne pepper.
3. After this, top the eggs with olives and close the lid.
4. Cook the eggs on High for 2 hours.

Nutrition Info:
- Per Serving: 165 calories, 11.2g protein, 1.6g carbohydrates, 12.9g fat, 0.5g fiber, 335mg cholesterol, 240mg sodium, 129mg potassium

Creamy Yogurt

Servings: 8 | Cooking Time: 10 Hours

Ingredients:
- 3 teaspoons gelatin
- ½ gallon milk
- 7 ounces plain yogurt
- 1 and ½ tablespoons vanilla extract
- ½ cup maple syrup

Directions:

1. Put the milk in your Crock Pot, cover and cook on Low for 3 hours.
2. In a bowl, mix 1 cup of hot milk from the Crock Pot with the gelatin, whisk well, pour into the Crock Pot, cover and leave aside for 2 hours.
3. Combine 1 cup of milk with the yogurt, whisk really well and pour into the pot.
4. Also add vanilla and maple syrup, stir, cover and cook on Low for 7 more hours.
5. Leave yogurt aside to cool down and serve it for breakfast.

Nutrition Info:

- calories 200, fat 4, fiber 5, carbs 10, protein 5

Apricot Butter

Servings:4 | Cooking Time: 7 Hours

Ingredients:

- 1 cup apricots, pitted, chopped
- 3 tablespoons butter
- 1 teaspoon ground cinnamon
- 1 teaspoon brown sugar

Directions:

1. Put all ingredients in the Crock Pot and stir well
2. Close the lid and cook them on Low for 7 hours.
3. Then blend the mixture with the help of the immersion blender and cool until cold.

Nutrition Info:

- Per Serving: 99 calories, 0.6g protein, 5.5g carbohydrates, 8.9g fat, 1.1g fiber, 23mg cholesterol, 62mg sodium, 106mg potassium.

Light Egg Scramble

Servings:2 | Cooking Time: 4 Hours

Ingredients:

- 1 tablespoon butter, melted
- 6 eggs, beaten
- 1 teaspoon salt
- 1 teaspoon ground paprika

Directions:

1. Pour the melted butter in the Crock Pot.
2. Add eggs and salt and stir.
3. Cook the eggs on Low for 4 hours. Stir the eggs every 15 minutes.
4. When the egg scramble is cooked, top it with ground paprika.

Nutrition Info:

- Per Serving: 243 calories, 16.8g protein, 1.6g carbohydrates, 19g fat, 0.4g fiber, 506mg cholesterol, 1389mg sodium, 203mg potassium

Chicken Meatballs

Servings:4 | Cooking Time: 4 Hours

Ingredients:

- 3 tablespoons bread crumbs
- 1 teaspoon cream cheese
- 10 oz ground chicken
- 1 tablespoon coconut oil
- 1 teaspoon Italian seasonings

Directions:

1. Mix bread crumbs with cream cheese, ground chicken, and Italian seasonings.
2. Make the meatballs and put them in the Crock Pot.
3. Add coconut oil and close the lid.
4. Cook the chicken meatballs for 4 hours on High.

Nutrition Info:

- Per Serving: 190 calories, 21.2g protein, 3.8g carbohydrates, 9.6g fat, 0.2g fiber, 65mg cholesterol, 101mg sodium, 184mg potassium.

Squash Bowls

Servings: 2 | Cooking Time: 6 Hours

Ingredients:

- 2 tablespoons walnuts, chopped
- 2 cups squash, peeled and cubed
- ½ cup coconut cream
- ½ teaspoon cinnamon powder
- ½ tablespoon sugar

Directions:

1. In your Crock Pot, mix the squash with the nuts and the other ingredients, toss, put the lid on and cook on Low for 6 hours.
2. Divide into bowls and serve.

Nutrition Info:

- calories 140, fat 1, fiber 2, carbs 2, protein 5

Omelet With Greens

Servings:2 | Cooking Time: 2 Hours

Ingredients:
- 3 eggs, beaten
- ¼ cup milk
- 1 cup baby arugula, chopped
- ½ teaspoon salt
- 1 teaspoon avocado oil

Directions:
1. In the bowl mix eggs with milk, salt, and arugula.
2. Then sprinkle the Crock Pot with avocado oil from inside.
3. Pour the omelet egg mixture in the Crock Pot and close the lid.
4. Cook the meal on High for 2 hours.

Nutrition Info:
- Per Serving: 115 calories, 9.6g protein, 2.5g carbohydrates, 7.6g fat, 0.3g fiber, 248mg cholesterol, 691mg sodium, 150mg potassium.

Ham Pockets

Servings:4 | Cooking Time: 1 Hour

Ingredients:
- 4 pita bread
- ½ cup Cheddar cheese, shredded
- 4 ham slices
- 1 tablespoon mayonnaise
- 1 teaspoon dried dill

Directions:
1. Mix cheese with mayonnaise and dill.
2. Then fill the pita bread with sliced ham and cheese mixture.
3. Wrap the stuffed pitas in the foil and place it in the Crock Pot.
4. Cook them on High for 1 hour.

Nutrition Info:
- Per Serving: 283 calories, 13.7g protein, 35.7g carbohydrates, 9.1g fat, 1.7g fiber, 32mg cholesterol, 801mg sodium, 175mg potassium.

Chicken Omelet

Servings:4 | Cooking Time: 3 Hours

Ingredients:
- 4 oz chicken fillet, boiled, shredded
- 1 tomato, chopped
- 4 eggs, beaten
- 1 tablespoon cream cheese
- 1 teaspoon olive oil

Directions:
1. Brush the Crock Pot bowl with olive oil from inside.
2. In the mixing bowl mix shredded chicken, tomato, eggs, and cream cheese.
3. Then pour the mixture in the Crock Pot bowl and close the lid.
4. Cook the omelet for 3 hours on Low.

Nutrition Info:
- Per Serving: 138 calories, 14.1g protein, 1g carbohydrates, 8.5g fat, 0.2g fiber, 192mg cholesterol, 94mg sodium, 168mg potassium.

Asparagus Egg Casserole

Servings:4 | Cooking Time: 2.5 Hours

Ingredients:
- 7 eggs, beaten
- 4 oz asparagus, chopped, boiled
- 1 oz Parmesan, grated
- 1 teaspoon sesame oil
- 1 teaspoon dried dill

Directions:
1. Pour the sesame oil in the Crock Pot.
2. Then mix dried dill with parmesan, asparagus, and eggs.
3. Pour the egg mixture in the Crock Pot and close the lid.
4. Cook the casserole on high for 2.5 hours.

Nutrition Info:
- Per Serving: 149 calories, 12.6g protein, 2.1g carbohydrates, 10.3g fat, 0.6g fiber, 292mg cholesterol, 175mg sodium, 169mg potassium

Crockpot Fisherman's Eggs

Servings: 2 | Cooking Time: 3 Hours

Ingredients:
- 1 can organic sardines in olive oil
- 2 organic eggs
- ½ cup arugula, rinsed and drained
- ½ of artichoke hearts, chopped
- Salt and pepper to taste

Directions:
1. Put the sardines in the bottom of the CrockPot.
2. Break the eggs on top of the sardines and add the arugula and artichokes on top.
3. Season with salt and pepper to taste.
4. Close the lid and cook on high for 2 hours or on low for 3 hours.

Nutrition Info:
- Calories per serving: 315; Carbohydrates: 3.5g; Protein: 28g; Fat: 20.6 g; Sugar: 0g; Sodium: 491mg; Fiber: 1.3g

Leek Eggs

Servings: 4 | Cooking Time: 2.5 Hours

Ingredients:
- 10 oz leek, sliced
- 4 eggs, beaten
- 1 teaspoon olive oil
- ½ teaspoon cumin seeds
- 3 oz Cheddar cheese, shredded

Directions:
1. Mix leek with olive oil and eggs.
2. Then transfer the mixture in the Crock Pot.
3. Sprinkle the egg mixture with Cheddar cheese and cumin seeds.
4. Close the lid and cook the meal on High for 2.5 hours.

Nutrition Info:
- Per Serving: 203 calories, 11.9g protein, 10.8g carbohydrates, 12.9g fat, 1.3g fiber, 186mg cholesterol, 208mg sodium, 212mg potassium

Giant Pancake

Servings: 4 | Cooking Time: 4 Hours

Ingredients:
- 1 cup pancake mix
- ½ cup milk
- 2 eggs, beaten
- 1 tablespoon coconut oil, melted

Directions:
1. Whisk pancake mix with milk, and eggs.
2. Then brush the Crock Pot mold with coconut oil from inside.
3. Pour the pancake mixture in the Crock Pot and close the lid.
4. Cook it on High for 4 hours.

Nutrition Info:
- Per Serving: 225 calories, 7.8g protein, 29.9g carbohydrates, 8.1g fat, 1g fiber, 94mg cholesterol, 529mg sodium, 7.8mg potassium.

Chapter 3 Appetizers Recipes

Chapter 3 Appetizers Recipes

Chipotle Bbq Sausage Bites

Servings: 10 | Cooking Time: 2 1/4 Hours

Ingredients:
- 3 pounds small smoked sausages
- 1 cup BBQ sauce
- 2 chipotle peppers in adobo sauce
- 1 tablespoon tomato paste
- 1/4 cup white wine
- Salt and pepper to taste

Directions:
1. Combine all the ingredients in your Crock Pot.
2. Add salt and pepper if needed and cover with a lid.
3. Cook on high settings for 2 hours.
4. Serve the sausage bites warm or chilled.

Bacon Chicken Sliders

Servings: 8 | Cooking Time: 4 1/2 Hours

Ingredients:
- 2 pounds ground chicken
- 1 egg
- 1/2 cup breadcrumbs
- 1 shallot, chopped
- Salt and pepper to taste
- 8 bacon slices

Directions:
1. Mix the chicken, egg, breadcrumbs and shallot in a bowl. Add salt and pepper to taste and give it a good mix.
2. Form small sliders then wrap each slider in a bacon slice.
3. Place the sliders in a Crock Pot.
4. Cover with its lid and cook on high settings for 4 hours, making sure to flip them over once during cooking.
5. Serve them warm.

Boiled Peanuts With Skin On

Servings: 8 | Cooking Time: 7 1/4 Hours

Ingredients:
- 2 pounds uncooked, whole peanuts
- 1/2 cup salt
- 4 cups water

Directions:
1. Combine all the ingredients in your Crock Pot.
2. Cover and cook on low settings for 7 hours.
3. Drain and allow to cool down before servings.

Maple Syrup Glazed Carrots

Servings: 8 | Cooking Time: 6 1/4 Hours

Ingredients:
- 3 pounds baby carrots
- 4 tablespoons butter, melted
- 3 tablespoons maple syrup
- 1/8 teaspoon pumpkin pie spices
- 1 teaspoon salt

Directions:
1. Place the baby carrots in your Crock Pot and add the remaining ingredients.
2. Mix until the carrots are evenly coated.
3. Cover and cook on low settings for 6 hours.
4. Serve the carrots warm or chilled.

Bacon Baked Potatoes

Servings: 8 | Cooking Time: 3 1/4 Hours

Ingredients:
- 3 pounds new potatoes, halved
- 8 slices bacon, chopped
- 1 teaspoon dried rosemary
- 1/4 cup chicken stock
- Salt and pepper to taste

Directions:
1. Heat a skillet over medium flame and stir in the bacon. Cook until crisp.
2. Place the potatoes in a Crock Pot. Add the bacon bits and its fat, as well as rosemary, salt and pepper and mix until evenly distributed.

3. Pour in the stock and cook on high heat for 3 hours.
4. Serve the potatoes warm.

Bacon New Potatoes

Servings: 6 | Cooking Time: 3 1/4 Hours

Ingredients:
- 3 pounds new potatoes, washed and halved
- 12 slices bacon, chopped
- 2 tablespoons white wine
- Salt and pepper to taste
- 1 rosemary sprig

Directions:
1. Place the potatoes, wine and rosemary in your Crock Pot.
2. Add salt and pepper to taste and top with chopped bacon.
3. Cook on high settings for 3 hours.
4. Serve the potatoes warm.

Cheesy Beef Dip

Servings: 8 | Cooking Time: 3 1/4 Hours

Ingredients:
- 2 pounds ground beef
- 1 pound grated Cheddar
- 1/2 cup cream cheese
- 1/2 cup white wine
- 1 poblano pepper, chopped

Directions:
1. Combine all the ingredients in a crock pot.
2. Cook on high settings for 3 hours.
3. Serve preferably warm.

French Onion Dip

Servings: 10 | Cooking Time: 4 1/4 Hours

Ingredients:
- 4 large onions, chopped
- 2 tablespoons olive oil
- 1 tablespoon butter
- 1 1/2 cups sour cream
- 1 pinch nutmeg
- Salt and pepper to taste

Directions:
1. Combine the onions, olive oil, butter, salt, pepper and nutmeg in a Crock Pot.

2. Cover and cook on high settings for 4 hours.
3. When done, allow to cool then stir in the sour cream and adjust the taste with salt and pepper.
4. Serve the dip right away.

Sausage Dip

Servings: 8 | Cooking Time: 6 1/4 Hours

Ingredients:
- 1 pound fresh pork sausages
- 1 pound spicy pork sausages
- 1 cup cream cheese
- 1 can diced tomatoes
- 2 poblano peppers, chopped

Directions:
1. Combine all the ingredients in a crock pot.
2. Cook on low settings for 6 hours.
3. Serve warm or chilled.

Bourbon Glazed Sausages

Servings: 10 | Cooking Time: 4 1/4 Hours

Ingredients:
- 3 pounds small sausage links
- 1/2 cup apricot preserves
- 1/4 cup maple syrup
- 2 tablespoons Bourbon

Directions:
1. Combine all the ingredients in your Crock Pot.
2. Cover with its lid and cook on low settings for 4 hours.
3. Serve the glazed sausages warm or chilled, preferably with cocktail sticks.

Bacon Wrapped Dates

Servings: 8 | Cooking Time: 1 3/4 Hours

Ingredients:
- 16 dates, pitted
- 16 almonds
- 16 slices bacon

Directions:
1. Stuff each date with an almond.
2. Wrap each date in bacon and place the wrapped dates in your Crock Pot.
3. Cover with its lid and cook on high settings for 1 1/4 hours.
4. Serve warm or chilled.

Cranberry Baked Brie

Servings: 6 | Cooking Time: 2 1/4 Hours

Ingredients:
- 1 wheel of Brie
- 1/2 cup cranberry sauce
- 1/2 teaspoon dried thyme

Directions:
1. Spoon the cranberry sauce in your Crock Pot.
2. Sprinkle with thyme and top with the Brie cheese.
3. Cover with a lid and cook on low settings for 2 hours.
4. The cheese is best served warm with bread sticks or tortilla chips.

Bacon Wrapped Chicken Livers

Servings: 6 | Cooking Time: 3 1/2 Hours

Ingredients:
- 2 pounds chicken livers
- Bacon slices as needed

Directions:
1. Wrap each chicken liver in one slice of bacon and place all the livers in your crock pot.
2. Cook on high heat for 3 hours.
3. Serve warm or chilled.

Chapter 4 Beef, Pork & Lamb Recipes

Chapter 4 Beef, Pork & Lamb Recipes

Blanked Hot Dogs

Servings:4 | Cooking Time: 4 Hours

Ingredients:
- 4 mini (cocktail) pork sausages
- 1 teaspoon cumin seeds
- 1 tablespoon olive oil
- 1 egg, beaten
- 4 oz puff pastry

Directions:
1. Roll up the puff pastry and cut into strips.
2. Put the pork sausages on every strip.
3. Roll the puff pastry and brush with egg.
4. Then top the blanked hot dogs with cumin seeds.
5. Brush the Crock Pot with olive oil from inside.
6. Add the blanked hot dogs and close the lid.
7. Cook them on high for 4 hours.

Nutrition Info:
- Per Serving: 225 calories, 4.4g protein, 14.1g carbohydrates, 16.9g fat, 0.6g fiber, 41mg cholesterol, 120mg sodium, 42mg potassium

Beef Brisket In Orange Juice

Servings:4 | Cooking Time: 5 Hours

Ingredients:
- 1 cup of orange juice
- 2 cups of water
- 2 tablespoons butter
- 12 oz beef brisket
- ½ teaspoon salt

Directions:
1. Toss butter in the skillet and melt.
2. Put the beef brisket in the melted butter and roast on high heat for 3 minutes per side.
3. Then sprinkle the meat with salt and transfer in the Crock Pot.
4. Add orange juice and water.
5. Close the lid and cook the meat on High for 5 hours.

Nutrition Info:
- Per Serving: 237 calories, 26.3g protein, 6.5g carbohydrates, 11.2g fat, 0.1g fiber, 91mg cholesterol, 392mg sodium, 470mg potassium.

Tenderloin Steaks With Red Wine And Mushrooms

Servings:4 | Cooking Time: 12 Hours

Ingredients:
- 4 pounds beef tenderloin steaks
- Salt and pepper to taste
- 1 package Portobello mushrooms, sliced
- 1 cup dry red wine
- 2 tablespoons butter

Directions:
1. Place all ingredients in the crockpot.
2. Give a good stir.
3. Close the lid and cook on low for 12 hours or on high for 10 hours.

Nutrition Info:
- Calories per serving: 415; Carbohydrates:7.2 g; Protein:30.3 g; Fat: 27.4g; Sugar: 0g; Sodium: 426mg; Fiber:3.8 g

Beef Sausages In Maple Syrup

Servings:4 | Cooking Time: 5 Hours

Ingredients:
- 1-pound beef sausages
- ½ cup maple syrup
- 3 tablespoons butter
- 1 teaspoon ground cumin
- ¼ cup of water

Directions:
1. Toss butter in the skillet and melt it.
2. Then pour the melted butter in the Crock Pot.
3. Add water, cumin, and maple syrup. Stir the liquid until smooth.
4. Add beef sausages and close the lid.
5. Cook the meal on High for 5 hours.

Nutrition Info:
- Per Serving: 630 calories, 15.8 g protein, 29.7g carbohydrates, 50g fat, 0.1g fiber, 103mg cholesterol, 979mg sodium, 307mg potassium.

Cayenne Pepper Strips

Servings:4 | Cooking Time: 4 Hours

Ingredients:
- 1-pound pork sirloin, cut into strips
- 1 teaspoon cayenne pepper
- 2 tablespoons ketchup
- 1 tablespoon avocado oil
- 1 cup of water

Directions:
1. Mix ketchup with cayenne pepper and avocado oil.
2. Then carefully brush the pork strips with ketchup mixture and put in the Crock Pot.
3. Add water and close the lid.
4. Cook the meat on high for 4 hours.

Nutrition Info:
- Per Serving: 204 calories, 23.3g protein, 2.3g carbohydrates, 10.6g fat, 0.3g fiber, 80mg cholesterol, 151mg sodium, 49mg potassium

Crockpot Cheeseburgers Casserole

Servings:4 | Cooking Time: 8 Hours

Ingredients:
- 1 white onion, chopped
- 1 ½ pounds lean ground beef
- 2 tablespoons mustard
- 1 teaspoon dried basil leaves
- 2 cups cheddar cheese

Directions:
1. Heat skillet over medium flame and sauté both white onions and ground beef for 3 minutes. Continue stirring until lightly brown.
2. Transfer to the crockpot and stir in mustard and basil leaves. Season with salt and pepper.
3. Add cheese on top.
4. Close the lid and cook on low for 8 hours and on high for 6 hours.

Nutrition Info:
- Calories per serving: 472; Carbohydrates: 3g; Protein: 32.7g; Fat: 26.2g; Sugar: 0g; Sodium: 429mg; Fiber: 2.4g

Beef Casserole

Servings:5 | Cooking Time: 7 Hours

Ingredients:
- 7 oz ground beef
- 1 cup Cheddar cheese, shredded
- ½ cup cream
- 1 teaspoon Italian seasonings
- ½ cup broccoli, chopped

Directions:
1. Mix ground beef with Italian seasonings and put in the Crock Pot.
2. Top the meat with broccoli and Cheddar cheese.
3. Then pour the cream over the casserole mixture and close the lid.
4. Cook the casserole on Low for 7 hours.

Nutrition Info:
- Per Serving: 186 calories, 18.1g protein, 1.7g carbohydrates, 11.6g fat, 0.2g fiber, 64mg cholesterol, 178mg sodium, 220mg potassium.

Seasoned Poached Pork Belly

Servings:4 | Cooking Time: 4 Hours

Ingredients:
- 10 oz pork belly
- 1 teaspoon minced garlic
- 1 teaspoon ginger paste
- ¼ cup apple cider vinegar
- 1 cup of water

Directions:
1. Rub the pork belly with minced garlic and garlic paste.
2. Then sprinkle it with apple cider vinegar and transfer in the Crock Pot.
3. Add water and close the lid.
4. Cook the pork belly on High for 4 hours.
5. Then slice the cooked pork belly and sprinkle with hot gravy from the Crock Pot.

Nutrition Info:
- Per Serving: 333 calories, 32.8g protein, 0.7g carbohydrates, 19.1g fat, 0.1g fiber, 82mg cholesterol, 1148mg sodium, 20mg potassium

Pesto Pork Chops

Servings:4 | Cooking Time: 8 Hours

Ingredients:
- 4 pork chops
- 4 teaspoons pesto sauce
- 4 tablespoons butter

Directions:
1. Brush pork chops with pesto sauce.
2. Put butter in the Crock Pot.
3. Add pork chops and close the lid.
4. Cook the meat on low for 8 hours.
5. Then transfer the cooked pork chops in the plates and sprinkle with butter-pesto gravy from the Crock Pot.

Nutrition Info:
- Per Serving: 380 calories, 18.6g protein, 0.3g carbohydrates, 33.6g fat, 0.1g fiber, 101mg cholesterol, 89mg sodium, 279mg potassium

Bacon Beef Strips

Servings:4 | Cooking Time: 5 Hours

Ingredients:
- 1-pound beef tenderloin, cut into strips
- 4 oz bacon, sliced
- 1 teaspoon salt
- ½ teaspoon ground black pepper
- ½ cup of water

Directions:
1. Mix beef with salt and ground black pepper.
2. Then wrap every beef strip with sliced bacon and arrange it in the Crock Pot.
3. Add water and close the lid.
4. Cook the meal on High for 5 hours.

Nutrition Info:
- Per Serving: 258 calories,28.9g protein, 0.4g carbohydrates, 14.8g fat, 0.1g fiber, 90mg cholesterol, 869mg sodium, 379mg potassium.

Basil Beef

Servings:4 | Cooking Time: 4 Hours

Ingredients:
- 1-pound beef loin, chopped
- 2 tablespoons dried basil
- 2 tablespoons butter
- ½ cup of water
- 1 teaspoon salt

Directions:
1. Toss the butter in the skillet and melt it.
2. Then mix the beef loin with dried basil and put in the hot butter.
3. Roast the meat for 2 minutes per side and transfer in the Crock Pot.
4. Add salt and water.
5. Close the lid and cook the beef on high for 4 hours.

Nutrition Info:
- Per Serving: 220 calories, 21g protein, 1.4g carbohydrates, 13.9g fat, 0g fiber, 76mg cholesterol, 1123mg sodium, 6mg potassium.

Kebab Cubes

Servings:4 | Cooking Time: 5 Hours

Ingredients:
- 1 teaspoon curry powder
- 1 teaspoon dried mint
- 1 teaspoon cayenne pepper
- ½ cup plain yogurt
- 1-pound beef tenderloin, cubed

Directions:
1. In the mixing bowl, mix beef cubes with plain yogurt, cayenne pepper, dried mint, and curry powder.
2. Then put the mixture in the Crock Pot. Add water if there is not enough liquid and close the lid.
3. Cook the meal on High for 5 hours.

Nutrition Info:
- Per Serving: 259 calories, 34.7g protein, 2.7g carbohydrates, 10.9g fat, 0.3g fiber, 106mg cholesterol, 89mg sodium, 495mg potassium.

Easy Crockpot Pulled Pork

Servings:4 | Cooking Time: 12 Hours

Ingredients:
- 4 pork shoulder, trimmed from excess fat
- 1 small onion, sliced
- Salt and pepper to taste
- 1 cup water
- 1 teaspoon rosemary

Directions:
1. Place all ingredients in the crockpot.
2. Cook on low for 12 hours or on high for 8 hours.

3. Once cooked, use forks to shred the meat.

Nutrition Info:
- Calories per serving: 533; Carbohydrates: 2g; Protein: 47.2g; Fat: 32.3g; Sugar: 0g; Sodium: 629mg; Fiber: 1.4g

Thyme Beef

Servings:2 | Cooking Time: 5 Hours

Ingredients:
- 8 oz beef sirloin, chopped
- 1 tablespoon dried thyme
- 1 tablespoon olive oil
- ½ cup of water
- 1 teaspoon salt

Directions:
1. Preheat the skillet well.
2. Then mix beef with dried thyme and olive oil.
3. Put the meat in the hot skillet and roast for 2 minutes per side on high heat.
4. Then transfer the meat in the Crock Pot.
5. Add salt and water.
6. Cook the meal on High for 5 hours.

Nutrition Info:
- Per Serving: 274 calories, 34.5g protein, 0.9g carbohydrates, 14.2g fat, 0.5g fiber, 101mg cholesterol, 1240mg sodium, 469mg potassium.

Roast With Pepperoncini

Servings: 4 | Cooking Time: 8 Hrs.

Ingredients:
- 5 lbs. beef chuck roast
- 1 tbsp soy sauce
- 10 pepperoncini's
- 1 cup beef stock
- 2 tbsp butter, melted

Directions:
1. Add beef roast and all other ingredients to the insert of Crock Pot.
2. Put the cooker's lid on and set the cooking time to 8 hours on Low settings.
3. Shred the cooked meat with the help of 2 forks and return to the cooker.
4. Mix gently and serve warm.

Nutrition Info:
- Per Serving: Calories: 362, Total Fat: 4g, Fiber: 8g, Total Carbs: 17g, Protein: 17g

Naked Beef Enchilada In A Crockpot

Servings:4 | Cooking Time: 6 Hours

Ingredients:
- 1-pound ground beef
- 2 tablespoons enchilada spice mix
- 1 cup cauliflower florets
- 2 cups Mexican cheese blend, grated
- ¼ cup cilantro, chopped

Directions:
1. In a skillet, sauté the ground beef over medium flame for 3 minutes.
2. Transfer to the crockpot and add the enchilada spice mix and cauliflower.
3. Stir to combine.
4. Add the Mexican cheese blend on top.
5. Cook on low for 6 hours or on high for 4 hours.
6. Sprinkle with cilantro on top.

Nutrition Info:
- Calories per serving: 481; Carbohydrates: 1g; Protein: 35.1g; Fat: 29.4g; Sugar: 0g; Sodium: 536mg; Fiber:0 g

Garlic Pork Ribs

Servings:3 | Cooking Time: 5.5 Hours

Ingredients:
- 8 oz pork ribs, chopped
- 1 teaspoon garlic powder
- 1 teaspoon avocado oil
- ½ teaspoon salt
- ½ cup of water

Directions:
1. Preheat the skillet until hot.
2. Then sprinkle the pork ribs with garlic powder and avocado oil and put in the hot skillet.
3. Roast the ribs for 3 minutes per side or until they are light brown.
4. Then transfer the pork ribs in the Crock Pot and sprinkle with salt.
5. Add water and cook the ribs on high for 5 hours.

Nutrition Info:
- Per Serving: 212 calories, 20.2g protein, 0.8g carbohydrates, 13.6g fat, 0.2g fiber, 78mg cholesterol, 433mg sodium, 233mg potassium.

Pepsi Pork Tenderloin

Servings:4 | Cooking Time: 6 Hours

Ingredients:
- 1-pound pork tenderloin
- 1 cup Pepsi
- 1 teaspoon cumin seeds
- 1 teaspoon olive oil
- 2 tablespoons soy sauce

Directions:

1. Chop the pork tenderloin roughly and put it in the mixing bowl.
2. Add cumin seeds, soy sauce, Pepsi, and olive oil. Leave the meat for 30 minutes to marinate.
3. After this, transfer the meat and all Pepsi liquid in the Crock Pot and close the lid.
4. Cook the meat on low for 6 hours.

Nutrition Info:
- Per Serving: 179 calories, 30.3g protein, 0.8g carbohydrates, 5.3g fat, 0.1g fiber,83mg cholesterol, 523mg sodium, 514mg potassium

Tender Butter Knuckle

Servings:4 | Cooking Time: 8 Hours

Ingredients:
- 1-pound pork knuckle
- 1/3 cup butter
- 1 teaspoon dried rosemary
- 1 teaspoon dried thyme
- ½ cup of coconut milk

Directions:

1. Mix the butter with dried rosemary and thyme.
2. Carefully rub the pork knuckle and put it in the Crock Pot.
3. Add coconut milk and close the lid.
4. Cook the meal on Low for 8 hours.

Nutrition Info:
- Per Serving: 448 calories, 33.2g protein, 2g carbohydrates, 34.1g fat, 0.9g fiber, 137mg cholesterol, 195mg sodium, 543mg potassium

Chili Beef Sausages

Servings:5 | Cooking Time: 4 Hours

Ingredients:
- 1-pound beef sausages
- 1 tablespoon olive oil
- ¼ cup of water
- 1 teaspoon chili powder

Directions:

1. Pour olive oil in the Crock Pot.
2. Then sprinkle the beef sausages with chili powder and put in the Crock Pot.
3. Add water and close the lid.
4. Cook the beef sausages on high for 4 hours.

Nutrition Info:
- Per Serving: 385 calories, 12.6g protein, 2.7g carbohydrates, 35.8g fat, 0.2g fiber, 64mg cholesterol, 736mg sodium, 182mg potassium.

Apple Pork

Servings:4 | Cooking Time: 8 Hours

Ingredients:
- 1-pound pork tenderloin, chopped
- 1 teaspoon ground cinnamon
- 1 tablespoon maple syrup
- 1 cup apples, chopped
- 1 cup of water

Directions:

1. Mix apples with ground cinnamon and put in the Crock Pot.
2. Add water, maple syrup, and pork tenderloin.
3. Close the lid and cook the meal on Low for 8 hours.

Nutrition Info:
- Per Serving: 206 calories, 29.9g protein, 11.5g carbohydrates, 4.1g fat, 1.7g fiber, 83mg cholesterol, 67mg sodium, 550mg potassium

Jamaican Pork Shoulder

Servings: 12 | Cooking Time: 7 Hrs.

Ingredients:
- ½ cup beef stock
- 1 tbsp olive oil
- ¼ cup keto Jamaican spice mix
- 4 lbs. pork shoulder

Directions:

1. Add pork, Jamaican spice mix and all other ingredients to the Crock Pot.
2. Put the cooker's lid on and set the cooking time to 7 hours on Low settings.
3. Slice the roast and serve warm.

Nutrition Info:
- Per Serving: Calories: 400, Total Fat: 6g, Fiber: 7g, Total Carbs: 10g, Protein: 25g

Chili Beef Strips

Servings:4 | Cooking Time: 6 Hours

Ingredients:
- 1-pound beef loin, cut into strips
- 1 chili pepper, chopped
- 2 tablespoons coconut oil
- 1 teaspoon salt
- 1 teaspoon chili powder

Directions:
1. Sprinkle the beef strips with salt and chili powder.
2. Then put the chili pepper in the Crock Pot.
3. Add coconut oil and beef strips.
4. Close the lid and cook the meal on Low for 6 hours.

Nutrition Info:
- Per Serving: 267 calories, 30.4g protein, 0.5g carbohydrates, 16.4g fat, 0.3g fiber, 81mg cholesterol, 650mg sodium, 401mg potassium.

Beef-stuffed Peppers

Servings:8 | Cooking Time:5 Hours

Ingredients:
- 1-pound lean ground beef
- 1 can tomatoes and chilies
- 1 teaspoon cumin
- 8 medium sweet peppers, top and seeds removed
- 2 cups Mexican cheese blend

Directions:
1. Heat skillet over medium flame and add the ground beef. Stir for 3 minutes until lightly brown.
2. Add the tomatoes and cumin. Turn off the heat and allow to cool.
3. Spoon the beef mixture into the sweet peppers. Top with the Mexican cheese blend.
4. Place inside the crockpot and close the lid.
5. Cook on low for 5 hours or on high for 3 hours.

Nutrition Info:

- Calories per serving: 301; Carbohydrates: 2.5g; Protein:29 g; Fat: 14g; Sugar:0.3 g; Sodium: 797mg; Fiber: 3g

Taco Pork

Servings:5 | Cooking Time: 5 Hours

Ingredients:
- 1-pound pork shoulder, chopped
- 1 tablespoon taco seasonings
- 1 tablespoon lemon juice
- 1 cup of water

Directions:
1. Mix pork shoulder with taco seasonings and place in the Crock Pot.
2. Add water and cook it on High for 5 hours.
3. After this, transfer the cooked meat in the bowl and shred gently with the help of the fork.
4. Add lemon juice and shake gently.

Nutrition Info:
- Per Serving: 274 calories, 21.1g protein, 1.7g carbohydrates, 19.4g fat, 0g fiber, 82mg cholesterol, 232mg sodium, 303mg potassium

Cheesy Pork Casserole

Servings:4 | Cooking Time: 10 Hours

Ingredients:
- 4 pork chops, bones removed and sliced
- 1 cauliflower head, cut into florets
- 1 cup chicken broth
- 1 teaspoon rosemary
- 2 cups cheddar cheese

Directions:
1. Arrange the pork chop slices in the crockpot,
2. Add in the cauliflower florets.
3. Pour the chicken broth and rosemary. Season with salt and pepper to taste.
4. Pour cheddar cheese on top.
5. Close the lid and cook on low for 10 hours.

Nutrition Info:
- Calories per serving: 417; Carbohydrates: 7g; Protein: 32.1g; Fat: 26.2g; Sugar: 0; Sodium: 846mg; Fiber: 5.3g

Chili Crockpot Brisket

Servings:4 | Cooking Time: 12 Hours

Ingredients:
- 4 pounds beef brisket
- 1 bottle chili sauce
- Salt and pepper to taste
- 1 cup onion, chopped
- 1/8 cup water

Directions:
1. Place all ingredients in the crockpot.
2. Give a good stir.
3. Close the lid and cook on low for 12 hours or on high for 10 hours.

Nutrition Info:
- Calories per serving: 634; Carbohydrates: 2.1g; Protein: 30.2g; Fat: 45.4g; Sugar:0 g; Sodium: 835mg; Fiber: 1.4g

Crockpot Pork Roast

Servings:4 | Cooking Time: 12 Hours

Ingredients:
- 1-pound pork loin roast, bones removed
- 3 tablespoons olive oil
- 1 teaspoon thyme leaves
- 1 teaspoon marjoram leaves
- ½ tablespoon dry mustard

Directions:
1. Line the bottom of the crockpot with foil.
2. Combine all ingredients in a bowl. Massage the pork to coat all surface with the spices.
3. Place in the crockpot and cook on low for 12 hours or on high for 8 hours.

Nutrition Info:
- Calories per serving: 414; Carbohydrates: 0.8g; Protein: 52.2; Fat: 37.1g; Sugar:0 g; Sodium: 724mg; Fiber: 0g

Crockpot Moroccan Beef

Servings:8 | Cooking Time: 10 Hours

Ingredients:
- 2 pounds beef roast, cut into strips
- ½ cup onions, sliced
- 4 tablespoons garam masala
- 1 teaspoon salt

- ½ cup bone broth

Directions:
1. Place all ingredients in the CrockPot.
2. Give a good stir.
3. Close the lid and cook on high for 8 hours or on low for 10 hours.

Nutrition Info:
- Calories per serving: 310; Carbohydrates: 0.7g; Protein: 30.3g; Fat: 25.5g; Sugar: 0g; Sodium: 682mg; Fiber: 0.5g

Bbq Beer Beef Tenderloin

Servings:4 | Cooking Time: 10 Hours

Ingredients:
- ¼ cup beer
- 1-pound beef tenderloin
- ½ cup BBQ sauce
- 1 teaspoon fennel seeds
- 1 teaspoon olive oil

Directions:
1. Mix BBQ sauce with beer, fennel seeds, and olive oil.
2. Pour the liquid in the Crock Pot.
3. Add beef tenderloin and close the lid.
4. Cook the meal on Low for 10 hours.

Nutrition Info:
- Per Serving: 299 calories, 33g protein, 12.1g carbohydrates, 11.7g fat, 0.4g fiber, 104mg cholesterol, 418mg sodium, 482mg potassium.

Mexican Bubble Pizza

Servings:6 | Cooking Time: 6 Hours

Ingredients:
- 1 ½ pound ground beef
- 1 tablespoon taco seasoning
- 2 cups cheddar cheese, shredded
- 1 cup mozzarella cheese
- 1 can condensed tomato soup

Directions:
1. Heat skillet over medium flame and brown the ground beef for a few minutes. Stir in taco seasoning.
2. Place the cheddar cheese into the crockpot.
3. Add the sautéed ground beef on top of the cheddar cheese.
4. Pour the tomato sauce.

5. Sprinkle with mozzarella cheese on top.
6. Close the lid and cook on low for 6 hours and on high for 4 hours.

Nutrition Info:
- Calories per serving: 643; Carbohydrates: 5g; Protein: 45g; Fat: 35g; Sugar:2.1 g; Sodium: 1870mg; Fiber: 2.6g

Pork Loin Roast In Crockpot

Servings:8 | Cooking Time: 12 Hours

Ingredients:
- 2 pounds pork loin
- 2 onions, chopped
- 3 cups homemade beef stock
- Salt and pepper to taste

Directions:
1. Place all ingredients in the CrockPot.
2. Give a good stir.
3. Close the lid and cook on high for 10 hours or on low for 12 hours.

Nutrition Info:
- Calories per serving: 282; Carbohydrates: 4.7g; Protein: 30.6g; Fat: 15.9g; Sugar: 0g; Sodium: 635mg; Fiber: 2.8g

Mustard Beef

Servings:4 | Cooking Time: 8 Hours

Ingredients:
- 1-pound beef sirloin, chopped
- 1 tablespoon capers, drained
- 1 cup of water
- 2 tablespoons mustard
- 1 tablespoon coconut oil

Directions:
1. Mix meat with mustard and leave for 10 minutes to marinate.
2. Then melt the coconut oil in the skillet.
3. Add meat and roast it for 1 minute per side on high heat.
4. After this, transfer the meat in the Crock Pot.
5. Add water and capers.
6. Cook the meal on Low for 8 hours.

Nutrition Info:
- Per Serving: 267 calories, 35.9g protein, 2.1g carbohydrates, 12.1g fat, 0.9g fiber, 101mg cholesterol, 140mg sodium, 496mg potassium.

Beef And Sauerkraut Bowl

Servings:4 | Cooking Time: 5 Hours

Ingredients:
- 1 cup sauerkraut
- 1-pound corned beef, chopped
- ¼ cup apple cider vinegar
- 1 cup of water

Directions:
1. Pour water and apple cider vinegar in the Crock Pot.
2. Add corned beef and cook it on High for 5 hours.
3. Then chop the meat roughly and put in the serving bowls.
4. Top the meat with sauerkraut.

Nutrition Info:
- Per Serving: 202 calories, 15.5g protein, 1.7g carbohydrates, 14.2g fat, 1g fiber, 71mg cholesterol, 1240mg sodium, 236mg potassium.

3-ingredients Beef Roast

Servings:6 | Cooking Time: 5 Hours

Ingredients:
- 2-pounds beef chuck roast, chopped
- 1 teaspoon ground cumin
- 1 cup of water

Directions:
1. Put all ingredients from the list above in the Crock Pot.
2. Close the lid and cook the meal on High for 5 hours.

Nutrition Info:
- Per Serving: 550 calories, 39.6g protein, 0.2g carbohydrates, 42.1g fat, 0g fiber, 156mg cholesterol, 99mg sodium, 351mg potassium.

Roast And Pepperoncinis

Servings: 4 | Cooking Time: 8 Hours

Ingredients:
- 5 pounds beef chuck roast
- 1 tablespoon soy sauce
- 10 pepperoncinis
- 1 cup beef stock
- 2 tablespoons butter, melted

Directions:

1. In your Crock Pot, mix beef roast with soy sauce, pepperoncinis, stock and butter, toss well, cover and cook on Low for 8 hours.
2. Transfer roast to a cutting board, shred using 2 forks, return to Crock Pot, toss, divide between plates and serve.

Nutrition Info:
- calories 362, fat 4, fiber 8, carbs 17, protein 17

Hot Lamb Strips

Servings: 6 | Cooking Time: 5 Hours

Ingredients:
- 14 oz lamb fillet, cut into strips
- 1 teaspoon cayenne pepper
- 2 tablespoons butter, melted
- 1 tablespoon hot sauce
- ½ cup of water

Directions:
1. Mix lamb strips with hot sauce and cayenne pepper.
2. Transfer them in the Crock Pot.
3. After this, add water and butter.
4. Close the lid and cook the lamb on High for 5 hours.

Nutrition Info:
- Per Serving: 158 calories, 18.7g protein, 0.2g carbohydrates, 8.8g fat, 0.1g fiber, 70mg cholesterol, 142mg sodium, 232mg potassium.

Bacon Swiss Pork Chops

Servings: 8 | Cooking Time: 10 Hours

Ingredients:
- 8 pork chops, bone in
- 2 tablespoons olive oil
- 4 cloves of garlic
- 12 bacon strips, cut in half
- 1 cup Swiss cheese, shredded

Directions:
1. Season the pork chops with salt and pepper to taste
2. In a skillet, heat the olive oil over medium flame and sauté the garlic until fragrant and slightly golden.
3. Transfer to the crockpot.
4. Wrap the bacon strips around the pork chops.
5. Place in the crockpot and sprinkle with shredded Swiss cheese.
6. Close the lid and cook on low for 10 hours or on high for 8 hours.

Nutrition Info:
- Calories per serving: 519; Carbohydrates: 0.5g; Protein: 42.3g; Fat: 40.2g; Sugar: 0g; Sodium: 732mg; Fiber: 0g

Pork Tenderloin And Apples

Servings: 4 | Cooking Time: 8 Hours

Ingredients:
- A pinch of nutmeg, ground
- 2 pounds pork tenderloin
- 4 apples, cored and sliced
- 2 tablespoons maple syrup

Directions:
1. Place apples in your Crock Pot, sprinkle nutmeg over them, add pork tenderloin, sprinkle some more nutmeg, drizzle the maple syrup, cover and cook on Low for 8 hours.
2. Slice pork tenderloin, divide it between plates and serve with apple slices and cooking juices.

Nutrition Info:
- calories 400, fat 4, fiber 5, carbs 12, protein 20

Barbecue Crockpot Meatloaf

Servings: 6 | Cooking Time: 10 Hours

Ingredients:
- 1-pound ground beef
- 1 cup cheddar cheese
- 2 eggs, beaten
- Salt and pepper to taste
- 2 tablespoon liquid smoke

Directions:
1. Place all ingredients in a mixing bowl.
2. Scoop the mixture into greased ramekins.
3. Place the ramekins inside the crockpot.
4. Pour water into the crockpot such that 1/8 of the ramekins are soaked.
5. Close the lid and cook on low for 10 hours or on high for 7 hours.

Nutrition Info:
- Calories per serving: 330; Carbohydrates: 2 g; Protein: 21 g; Fat: 17 g; Sugar: 0g; Sodium: 668mg; Fiber: 0.7g

Rosemary And Bacon Pork Chops

Servings:4 | Cooking Time: 4 Hours

Ingredients:
- 4 pork chops
- 4 bacon slices
- 1 teaspoon dried rosemary
- 1 tablespoon olive oil
- ½ cup of water

Directions:
1. Rub the pork chops with rosemary and olive oil.
2. Then wrap the pork chops in the bacon and put in the hot skillet.
3. Roast the pork chops for 1 minute per side.
4. Then transfer them in the Crock Pot. Add water.
5. Close the lid and cook the meat on High for 4 hours.

Nutrition Info:
- Per Serving: 390 calories, 25g protein, 0.5g carbohydrates, 31.4g fat, 0.1g fiber, 90mg cholesterol, 496mg sodium, 386mg potassium

Succulent Pork Ribs

Servings:4 | Cooking Time: 8 Hours

Ingredients:
- 12 oz pork ribs, roughly chopped
- ¼ cup of orange juice
- 1 cup of water
- 1 teaspoon ground nutmeg
- 1 teaspoon salt

Directions:
1. Pour water and orange juice in the Crock Pot.
2. Then sprinkle the pork ribs with ground nutmeg and salt.
3. Put the pork ribs in the Crock Pot and close the lid.
4. Cook the meat on low for 8 hours.

Nutrition Info:
- Per Serving: 242 calories, 22.7g protein, 1.9g carbohydrates, 15.3g fat, 0.1g fiber, 88mg cholesterol, 633mg sodium, 279mg potassium

Flank Steak With Arugula

Servings:4 | Cooking Time: 10 Hours

Ingredients:
- 1-pound flank steak
- 1 teaspoon Worcestershire sauce
- Salt and pepper to taste
- 1 package arugula salad mix
- 2 tablespoon balsamic vinegar

Directions:
1. Season the flank steak with Worcestershire sauce, salt, and pepper.
2. Place in the crockpot that has been lined with aluminum foil.
3. Close the lid and cook on low for 10 hours or on high for 7 hours.
4. Meanwhile, prepare the salad by combining the arugula salad mix and balsamic vinegar. Set aside in the fridge.
5. Once the steak is cooked, allow to cool before slicing.
6. Serve on top of the arugula salad.

Nutrition Info:
- Calories per serving: 452; Carbohydrates: 5.8g; Protein: 30.2g; Fat:29.5g; Sugar: 1.2g; Sodium: 563mg; Fiber:3 g

Pan "grilled" Flank Steak

Servings:4 | Cooking Time: 10 Hours

Ingredients:
- 1 ½ pounds flank steak, fat trimmed
- Salt and pepper to taste
- A pinch of rosemary
- 1 tablespoon butter, melted
- 1 tablespoon parsley, chopped

Directions:
1. Season the flank steak with salt and pepper to taste.
2. Rub with a pinch of rosemary.
3. Pour the butter in the crockpot and add the slices of flank steak.
4. Close the lid and cook on low for 10 hours or on high for 8 hours.
5. Garnish with parsley before serving.

Nutrition Info:
- Calories per serving: 397; Carbohydrates: 1g; Protein:26.3 g; Fat: 20.7g; Sugar: 0g; Sodium:644mg; Fiber: 0.3g

Chili Beef Ribs

Servings:4 | Cooking Time: 5 Hours

Ingredients:
- 10 oz beef ribs, chopped
- 1 teaspoon hot sauce
- 1 teaspoon chili powder
- 1 tablespoon sesame oil
- ½ cup of water

Directions:
1. Mix the beef ribs with chili powder.
2. Then heat the sesame oil in the skillet until hot.
3. Add beef ribs and roast them for 2-3 minutes per side or until they are light brown.
4. After this, transfer the beef ribs in the Crock Pot.
5. Add water and hot sauce.
6. Close the lid and cook them on High for 5 hours.

Nutrition Info:
- Per Serving: 164 calories, 21.6g protein, 0.4g carbohydrates, 7.9g fat, 0.2g fiber, 63mg cholesterol, 86mg sodium, 300mg potassium.

Old Fashioned Shredded Beef

Servings:4 | Cooking Time: 6 Hours

Ingredients:
- ½ cup of canned soup
- 1 cup of water
- 1-pound beef tenderloin
- 1 teaspoon peppercorns

Directions:
1. Pour water in the Crock Pot.
2. Add peppercorns and beef tenderloin.
3. Close the lid and cook the meat on High for 5 hours.
4. After this, drain water and shred the meat with the help of the forks.
5. Add canned soup and stir well.
6. Cook the beef on High for 1 hour.

Nutrition Info:
- Per Serving: 247 calories, 33.4g protein, 1.8g carbohydrates, 10.9g fat, 0.1g fiber, 106mg cholesterol, 291mg sodium, 427mg potassium.

Hot Beef

Servings:4 | Cooking Time: 8 Hours

Ingredients:
- 1-pound beef sirloin, chopped
- 2 tablespoons hot sauce
- 1 tablespoon olive oil
- ½ cup of water

Directions:
1. In the shallow bowl mix hot sauce with olive oil.
2. Then mix beef sirloin with hot sauce mixture and leave for 10 minutes to marinate.
3. Put the marinated beef in the Crock Pot.
4. Add water and close the lid.
5. Cook the meal on Low for 8 hours.

Nutrition Info:
- Per Serving: 241 calories, 34.4g protein, 0.1g carbohydrates, 10.6g fat, 0g fiber, 101mg cholesterol, 266mg sodium, 467mg potassium.

Cajun Beef

Servings:4 | Cooking Time: 5 Hours

Ingredients:
- 1-pound beef ribs
- 1 tablespoon Cajun seasonings
- 3 tablespoons lemon juice
- 1 tablespoon coconut oil, melted
- ½ cup of water

Directions:
1. Rub the beef ribs with Cajun seasonings and sprinkle with lemon juice.
2. Then pour the coconut oil in the Crock Pot.
3. Add beef ribs and water.
4. Close the lid and cook the beef on high for 5 hours.

Nutrition Info:
- Per Serving: 243 calories, 34.5g protein, 0.2g carbohydrates, 10.6g fat, 0.1g fiber, 101mg cholesterol, 115mg sodium, 471mg potassium.

Lamb Chops

Servings:4 | Cooking Time: 5 Hours

Ingredients:
- 1 teaspoon ground black pepper
- ½ teaspoon salt
- 1 teaspoon sesame oil
- 4 lamb chops
- 1/3 cup water

Directions:
1. Sprinkle the lamb chops with sesame oil, salt, and ground black pepper.
2. Place the lamb chops in the Crock Pot and add water.
3. Close the lid and cook the meal on High for 5 hours.

Nutrition Info:
- Per Serving: 169 calories, 23.9g protein, 0.3g carbohydrates, 7.4g fat, 0.1g fiber, 77mg cholesterol, 356mg sodium, 292mg potassium.

Easy Pork Chop Dinner

Servings:4 | Cooking Time: 10 Hours

Ingredients:
- 2 teaspoons olive oil
- 2 cloves of garlic, chopped
- 1 onion, chopped
- 4 pork cops
- 2 cups chicken broth

Directions:
1. In a skillet, heat the oil and sauté the garlic and onions until fragrant and lightly golden. Add in the pork chops and cook for 2 minutes for 2 minutes on each side.
2. Pour the chicken broth and scrape the bottom to remove the browning.
3. Transfer to the crockpot. Season with salt and pepper to taste.
4. Close the lid and cook on low for 10 hours or on high for 7 hours.

Nutrition Info:
- Calories per serving: 481; Carbohydrates: 2.5g; Protein: 38.1g; Fat: 30.5g; Sugar: 0.3g; Sodium: 735mg; Fiber: 1.2g

Crockpot Pulled Pork

Servings:4 | Cooking Time: 12 Hours

Ingredients:
- 2 onions, cut into slices
- 1-pound pork shoulder roast, bones removed
- 2 tablespoons garlic powder
- Salt and pepper to taste
- 2 cups chicken broth

Directions:
1. Place all ingredients in the crockpot.
2. Close the lid and cook on low for 12 hours or on high for 10 hours.
3. Once cooked, take the meat out from the crockpot and shred using two forks.
4. Place the shredded meat back into the crockpot and allow to simmer for another two hours or until the meat is soaked in its juices.

Nutrition Info:
- Calories per serving:492; Carbohydrates: 1g; Protein: 36.1g; Fat: 29.5g; Sugar:0 g; Sodium:524 mg; Fiber: 0.7g

Tender Pork Chops

Servings: 4 | Cooking Time: 8 Hours

Ingredients:
- 2 yellow onions, chopped
- 6 bacon slices, chopped
- ½ cup chicken stock
- Salt and black pepper to the taste
- 4 pork chops

Directions:
1. In your Crock Pot, mix onions with bacon, stock, salt, pepper and pork chops, cover and cook on Low for 8 hours.
2. Divide pork chops on plates, drizzle cooking juices all over and serve.

Nutrition Info:
- calories 325, fat 18, fiber 1, carbs 12, protein 36

Oregano Pork Strips

Servings:4 | Cooking Time: 7 Hours

Ingredients:
- 12 oz pork tenderloin, cut into strips
- 1 tablespoon dried oregano
- 1 cup of water
- 1 teaspoon salt

Directions:
1. Place pork strips in the Crock Pot.
2. Add all remaining ingredients and close the lid.
3. Cook the pork strips on Low for 7 hours.
4. Serve the cooked meal with hot gravy from the Crock Pot.

Nutrition Info:
- Per Serving: 125 calories, 22.4g protein, 0.7g carbohydrates, 3.1g fat, 0.5g fiber, 62mg cholesterol, 632mg sodium, 378mg potassium

Dijon Basil Pork Loin

Servings:4 | Cooking Time: 10 Hours

Ingredients:
- 1 pork loin roast, trimmed from excess fat
- 2 tablespoons Dijon mustard
- 1 teaspoon marjoram
- Salt and pepper to taste
- ¼ cup basil, chopped

Directions:
1. Rub the pork loin roast with mustard, marjoram, salt and pepper.
2. Use your hands to massage the pork.
3. Place in the crockpot and sprinkle with chopped basil.
4. Close the lid and cook on low for 10 hours or on high for 8 hours.

Nutrition Info:
- Calories per serving: 449; Carbohydrates: 3g; Protein: 38.2g; Fat:33.1g; Sugar:0 g; Sodium: 764mg; Fiber: 1.3g

Bbq Bratwurst

Servings:5 | Cooking Time: 4 Hours

Ingredients:
- 1-pound bratwurst
- 4 tablespoons BBQ sauce
- 1 teaspoon olive oil
- ¼ cup of water
- 1 teaspoon chili powder

Directions:
1. Roast the bratwurst in the olive oil for 1 minute per side.
2. Then transfer the bratwurst in the Crock Pot.
3. Add water and BBQ sauce.
4. Close the lid and cook the meal on High for 4 hours.

Nutrition Info:
- Per Serving: 330 calories, 12.5g protein, 7.4g carbohydrates, 27.5g fat, 0.3g fiber, 67mg cholesterol, 913mg sodium, 352mg potassium.

Pork With Apples

Servings: 4 | Cooking Time: 8 Hrs.

Ingredients:
- A pinch of nutmeg, ground
- 2 lbs. pork tenderloin
- 4 apples, cored and sliced
- 2 tbsp maple syrup

Directions:
1. Add apples to the insert of the Crock Pot.
2. Drizzle nutmeg over the apples then add pork along with remaining ingredients.
3. Put the cooker's lid on and set the cooking time to 8 hours on Low settings.
4. Slice the pork and return to the apple mixture.
5. Mix well and serve warm.

Nutrition Info:
- Per Serving: Calories: 400, Total Fat: 4g, Fiber: 5g, Total Carbs: 12g, Protein: 20g

Salsa Meat

Servings:4 | Cooking Time: 4 Hours

Ingredients:
- 1-pound pork sirloin, sliced
- 1 cup tomatillo salsa
- 2 garlic cloves, diced
- 1 teaspoon apple cider vinegar
- ½ cup of water

Directions:
1. Put all ingredients in the Crock Pot and carefully mix.
2. Then close the lid and cook the salsa meat on high for 4 hours.

Nutrition Info:
- Per Serving: 214 calories, 23.8g protein, 2.3g carbohydrates, 11.2g fat, 0.4g fiber, 71mg cholesterol, 169mg sodium, 75mg potassium

5-ingredients Chili

Servings:4 | Cooking Time: 5 Hours

Ingredients:
- 8 oz ground beef
- ½ cup Cheddar cheese, shredded
- 2 cup tomatoes, chopped
- 1 teaspoon chili seasonings
- ½ cup of water

Directions:
1. Mix the ground beef with chili seasonings and transfer in the Crock Pot.
2. Add tomatoes and water.
3. Close the lid and cook the chili on high for 3 hours.
4. After this, open the lid and mix the chili well. Top it with cheddar cheese and close the lid.
5. Cook the chili on low for 2 hours more.

Nutrition Info:
- Per Serving: 180 calories, 21.6g protein, 4g carbohydrates, 8.4g fat, 1.1g fiber, 66mg cholesterol, 150mg sodium, 456mg potassium.

Simple Pork Chop Casserole

Servings:4 | Cooking Time: 10 Hours

Ingredients:
- 4 pork chops, bones removed and cut into bite-sized pieces
- 3 tablespoons minced onion
- ½ cup water
- Salt and pepper to taste
- 1 cup heavy cream

Directions:
1. Place the pork chop slices, onions, and water in the crockpot.
2. Season with salt and pepper to taste.
3. Close the lid and cook on low for 10 hours or on high for 8 hours.
4. Halfway through the cooking time, pour in the heavy cream.

Nutrition Info:
- Calories per serving: 515; Carbohydrates: 2.5g; Protein: 39.2g; Fat: 34.3g; Sugar: 0g; Sodium: 613mg; Fiber:0.9 g

Skirt Steak With Red Pepper Sauce

Servings:4 | Cooking Time: 12 Hours

Ingredients:
- 2 red bell peppers, chopped
- 2 tablespoons olive oil
- 1 teaspoon thyme leaves
- 1-pound skirt steak, sliced into 1 inch thick
- Salt and pepper to taste

Directions:
1. In a food processor, mix together the red bell peppers, olive oil, and thyme leaves. Blend until smooth. Add water to make the mixture slightly runny. Set aside.
2. Season the skirt steak with salt and pepper.
3. Place in the crockpot and pour over the pepper sauce.
4. Add more salt and pepper if desired.
5. Close the lid and cook on low for 12 hours or on high for 10 hours.

Nutrition Info:
- Calories per serving: 396; Carbohydrates:4 g; Protein: 32.5g; Fat: 21g; Sugar: 0g; Sodium: 428mg; Fiber: 2.8g

Chapter 5 Poultry Recipes

Chapter 5 Poultry Recipes

Sweet Chicken Mash

Servings:6 | Cooking Time: 7 Hours

Ingredients:
- 3 tablespoons maple syrup
- 1-pound ground chicken
- 1 teaspoon dried dill
- 1 cup Cheddar cheese, shredded
- 1 cup of water

Directions:
1. Put all ingredients in the Crock Pot and carefully mix.
2. Close the lid and cook the mash on Low for 7 hours.

Nutrition Info:
- Per Serving: 246 calories, 26.6g protein, 7g carbohydrates, 11.9g fat, 0g fiber, 87mg cholesterol, 184mg sodium, 229mg potassium.

Chicken Piccata

Servings:4 | Cooking Time: 8 Hours

Ingredients:
- 4 chicken breasts, skin and bones removed
- Salt and pepper to taste
- ¼ cup butter, cubed
- ¼ cup chicken broth
- 1 tablespoon lemon juice

Directions:
1. Place all ingredients in the crockpot.
2. Give a good stir to combine everything.
3. Close the lid and cook on low for 8 hours or on high for 6 hours.

Nutrition Info:
- Calories per serving: 265; Carbohydrates:2.3 g; Protein:24 g; Fat: 14g; Sugar: 0g; Sodium:442 mg; Fiber:0 g

Continental Beef Chicken

Servings:5 | Cooking Time: 9 Hours

Ingredients:
- 6 oz. dried beef
- 12 oz. chicken breast, diced
- 7 oz. sour cream
- 1 can onion soup
- 3 tbsp flour

Directions:
1. Spread half of the dried beef in the Crock Pot.
2. Top it with chicken breast, sour cream, onion soup, and flour.
3. Spread the remaining dried beef on top.
4. Put the cooker's lid on and set the cooking time to 9 hours on Low settings.
5. Serve warm.

Nutrition Info:
- Per Serving: Calories: 285, Total Fat: 15.1g, Fiber: 1g, Total Carbs: 12.56g, Protein: 24g

Orange Chicken(2)

Servings:4 | Cooking Time: 7 Hours

Ingredients:
- 1-pound chicken fillet, roughly chopped
- 4 oranges, peeled, chopped
- 1 cup of water
- 1 teaspoon peppercorns
- 1 onion, diced

Directions:
1. Put chicken and oranges in the Crock Pot.
2. Add water, peppercorns, and onion.
3. Close the lid and cook the meal on Low for 7 hours.

Nutrition Info:
- Per Serving: 314 calories, 34.9g protein, 24.5g carbohydrates, 8.7g fat, 5.2g fiber, 101mg cholesterol, 101mg sodium, 656mg potassium.

Chicken Parm

Servings:3 | Cooking Time: 4 Hours

Ingredients:
- 9 oz chicken fillet
- 1/3 cup cream
- 3 oz Parmesan, grated
- 1 teaspoon olive oil

Directions:
1. Brush the Crock Pot bowl with olive oil from inside.
2. Then slice the chicken fillet and place it in the Crock Pot.
3. Top it with Parmesan and cream.
4. Close the lid and cook the meal on High for 4 hours.

Nutrition Info:
- Per Serving: 283 calories, 33.9g protein, 1.8g carbohydrates, 15.4g fat, 0g fiber, 101mg cholesterol, 345mg sodium, 216mg potassium.

French-style Chicken

Servings:4 | Cooking Time: 7 Hours

Ingredients:
- 1 can onion soup
- 4 chicken drumsticks
- ½ cup celery stalk, chopped
- 1 teaspoon dried tarragon
- ¼ cup white wine

Directions:
1. Put ingredients in the Crock Pot and carefully mix them.
2. Then close the lid and cook the chicken on low for 7 hours.

Nutrition Info:
- Per Serving: 127 calories, 15.1g protein, 5.8g carbohydrates, 3.7g fat, 0.7g fiber, 40mg cholesterol, 688mg sodium, 185mg potassium.

Chicken And Sour Cream

Servings: 4 | Cooking Time: 4 Hours

Ingredients:
- 4 chicken thighs
- Salt and black pepper to the taste
- 1 teaspoon onion powder
- ¼ cup sour cream
- 2 tablespoons sweet paprika

Directions:
1. In a bowl, mix paprika with salt, pepper and onion powder and stir.
2. Season chicken pieces with this paprika mix, place them in your Crock Pot, add sour cream, toss, cover and cook on High for 4 hours.
3. Divide everything between plates and serve.

Nutrition Info:
- calories 384, fat 31, fiber 2, carbs 11, protein 33

Rosemary Rotisserie Chicken

Servings:12 | Cooking Time: 12 Hours

Ingredients:
- 1-gallon water
- ¾ cup salt
- ½ cup butter
- 2 tablespoons rosemary and other herbs of your choice
- 1 whole chicken, excess fat removed

Directions:
1. In a pot, combine the water, salt, sugar, and herbs.
2. Stir to dissolve the salt and sugar.
3. Submerge the chicken completely and allow to sit in the brine for 12 hours inside the fridge.
4. Line the crockpot with tin foil.
5. Place the chicken and cook on low for 12 hours or on high for 7 hours.

Nutrition Info:
- Calories per serving: 194; Carbohydrates: 1.4g; Protein:20.6 g; Fat:6.2g; Sugar: 0g; Sodium: 562mg; Fiber: 0.9g

Stuffed Chicken Fillets

Servings:6 | Cooking Time: 4 Hours

Ingredients:
- ½ cup green peas, cooked
- ½ cup long-grain rice, cooked
- 16 oz chicken fillets
- 1 cup of water
- 1 teaspoon Italian seasonings

Directions:
1. Make the horizontal cuts in chicken fillets.
2. After this, mix Italian seasonings with rice and green peas.
3. Fill the chicken fillet with rice mixture and secure them with toothpicks.
4. Put the chicken fillets in the Crock Pot.
5. Add water and close the lid.
6. Cook the chicken on high for 4 hours.

Nutrition Info:
- Per Serving: 212 calories, 23.6g protein, 14.2g carbohydrates, 6g fat, 0.8g fiber, 68mg cholesterol, 68mg sodium, 232mg potassium.

Tomato Chicken Sausages

Servings:4 | Cooking Time: 2 Hours

Ingredients:
- 1-pound chicken sausages
- 1 cup tomato juice
- 1 tablespoon dried sage
- 1 teaspoon salt
- 1 teaspoon olive oil

Directions:
1. Heat the olive oil in the skillet well.
2. Add chicken sausages and roast them for 1 minute per side on high heat.
3. Then transfer the chicken sausages in the Crock Pot.
4. Add all remaining ingredients and close the lid.
5. Cook the chicken sausages on High for 2 hours.

Nutrition Info:
- Per Serving: 236 calories, 15.3g protein, 10.5g carbohydrates, 13.7g fat, 1.1g fiber, 0mg cholesterol, 1198mg sodium, 145mg potassium.

Creamy Chicken

Servings: 4 | Cooking Time: 4 Hrs

Ingredients:
- 4 chicken thighs
- Salt and black pepper to the taste
- 1 tsp onion powder
- ¼ cup sour cream
- 2 tbsp sweet paprika

Directions:
1. Add chicken, paprika, salt, black pepper, onion powder, and sour cream to the Crock Pot.
2. Put the cooker's lid on and set the cooking time to 4 hours on High settings.
3. Serve warm.

Nutrition Info:
- Per Serving: Calories: 384, Total Fat: 31g, Fiber: 2g, Total Carbs: 11g, Protein: 33g

Halved Chicken

Servings:4 | Cooking Time: 5 Hours

Ingredients:
- 2-pounds whole chicken, halved
- 1 tablespoon salt
- 1 teaspoon ground black pepper
- 2 tablespoons mayonnaise
- ½ cup of water

Directions:
1. Mix the ground black pepper with salt and mayonnaise.
2. Then rub the chicken halves with mayonnaise mixture and transfer in the Crock Pot.
3. Add water and close the lid.
4. Cook the chicken on High for 5 hours.

Nutrition Info:
- Per Serving: 461 calories, 65.7g protein, 2.1g carbohydrates, 19.3g fat, 1.2g fiber, 0.1mg cholesterol, 1993mg sodium, 559mg potassium.

Spicy Almond-crusted Chicken Nuggets In The Crockpot

Servings:6 | Cooking Time: 8 Hours

Ingredients:
- ¼ cup butter, melted
- 1 ½ cups almond meal
- 1 ½ cups grated parmesan cheese
- 1 ½ pounds boneless chicken breasts, cut into strips
- 2 eggs, beaten

Directions:
1. Place foil at the bottom of the crockpot.
2. Combine the almond meal and parmesan cheese.
3. Dip the chicken strips into the eggs and dredge into the parmesan and cheese mixture.
4. Place carefully in the crockpot.
5. Close the lid and cook on low for 8 hours or on high for 6 hours.

Nutrition Info:
- Calories per serving: 371; Carbohydrates: 2.5g; Protein:29 g; Fat: 22g; Sugar: 0.8g; Sodium: 527mg; Fiber: 1.4g

Harissa Chicken Breasts

Servings:6 | Cooking Time: 8 Hours

Ingredients:
- 1 tablespoon olive oil
- 1-pound chicken breasts, skin and bones removed
- Salt to taste
- 2 tablespoon Harissa or Sriracha sauce
- 2 tablespoons toasted sesame seeds

Directions:
1. Pour oil in the crockpot.
2. Arrange the chicken breasts and season with salt and pepper to taste
3. Stir in the Sriracha or Harissa sauce. Give a good stir to incorporate everything.
4. Close the lid and cook on low for 8 hours or on high for 6 hours.
5. Once cooked, sprinkle toasted sesame seeds on top.

Nutrition Info:
- Calories per serving: 167; Carbohydrates: 1.1g; Protein: 16.3g; Fat: 10.6g; Sugar: 0g; Sodium: 632mg; Fiber: 0.6g

Chicken Enchilada

Servings:10 | Cooking Time: 8 Hours

Ingredients:
- 4 ½ cups shredded chicken
- 1 ¼ cup sour cream
- 1 can sugar-free green enchilada sauce
- 4 cups Monterey jack cheese
- ½ cup cilantro, chopped

Directions:
1. Place the shredded chicken in the crockpot.
2. Add in the sour cream and enchilada sauce.
3. Sprinkle with Monterey jack cheese.
4. Close the lid and cook on low for 8 hours or on high for 6 hours.
5. An hour before the cooking time ends, sprinkle with cilantro.

Nutrition Info:
- Calories per serving: 469; Carbohydrates: 5g; Protein: 34g; Fat:29 g; Sugar:2.2 g; Sodium: 977mg; Fiber: 1g

Garlic Duck

Servings:4 | Cooking Time: 5 Hours

Ingredients:
- 1-pound duck fillet
- 1 tablespoon minced garlic
- 1 tablespoon butter, softened
- 1 teaspoon dried thyme
- 1/3 cup coconut cream

Directions:
1. Mix minced garlic with butter, and dried thyme.
2. Then rub the suck fillet with garlic mixture and place it in the Crock Pot.
3. Add coconut cream and cook the duck on High for 5 hours.
4. Then slice the cooked duck fillet and sprinkle it with hot garlic coconut milk.

Nutrition Info:
- Per Serving: 216 calories, 34.1g protein, 2g carbohydrates, 8.4g fat, 0.6g fiber, 8mg cholesterol, 194mg sodium, 135mg potassium

Lemon Garlic Dump Chicken

Servings:6 | Cooking Time: 8 Hours

Ingredients:
- ¼ cup olive oil
- 2 teaspoon garlic, minced
- 6 chicken breasts, bones removed
- 1 tablespoon parsley, chopped
- 2 tablespoons lemon juice, freshly squeezed

Directions:
1. Heat oil in a skillet over medium flame.
2. Sauté the garlic until golden brown.
3. Arrange the chicken breasts in the crockpot.
4. Pour over the oil with garlic.
5. Add the parsley and lemon juice. Add a little water.
6. Close the lid and cook on low for 8 hours or on high for 6 hours.

Nutrition Info:
- Calories per serving: 581; Carbohydrates: 0.7g; Protein: 60.5g; Fat: 35.8g; Sugar: 0g; Sodium: 583mg; Fiber: 0.3g

Chicken Pate

Servings:6 | Cooking Time: 8 Hours

Ingredients:
- 1 carrot, peeled
- 1 teaspoon salt
- 1-pound chicken liver
- 2 cups of water
- 2 tablespoons coconut oil

Directions:
1. Chop the carrot roughly and put it in the Crock Pot.
2. Add chicken liver and water.
3. Cook the mixture for 8 hours on Low.
4. Then drain water and transfer the mixture in the blender.
5. Add coconut oil and salt.
6. Blend the mixture until smooth.
7. Store the pate in the fridge for up to 7 days.

Nutrition Info:
- Per Serving: 169 calories, 18.6g protein, 1.7g carbohydrates, 9.5g fat, 0.3g fiber, 426mg cholesterol, 454mg sodium, 232mg potassium.

Buffalo Chicken Tenders

Servings:4 | Cooking Time: 3.5 Hours

Ingredients:
- 12 oz chicken fillet
- 3 tablespoons buffalo sauce
- ½ cup of coconut milk
- 1 jalapeno pepper, chopped

Directions:
1. Cut the chicken fillet into tenders and sprinkle the buffalo sauce.
2. Put the chicken tenders in the Crock Pot.
3. Add coconut milk and jalapeno pepper.
4. Close the lid and cook the meal on high for 3.5 hours.

Nutrition Info:
- Per Serving: 235 calories, 25.3g protein, 2.4g carbohydrates, 13.5g fat, 1g fiber, 76mg cholesterol, 318mg sodium, 293mg potassium.

Horseradish Chicken Wings

Servings:4 | Cooking Time: 6 Hours

Ingredients:
- 3 tablespoons horseradish, grated
- 1 teaspoon ketchup
- 1 tablespoon mayonnaise
- ½ cup of water
- 1-pound chicken wings

Directions:
1. Mix chicken wings with ketchup, horseradish, and mayonnaise,
2. Put them in the Crock Pot and add water.
3. Cook the meal on Low for 6 hours.

Nutrition Info:
- Per Serving: 236 calories, 33g protein, 2.5g carbohydrates, 9.7g fat, 0.4g fiber, 102mg cholesterol, 174mg sodium, 309mg potassium.

Italian Style Tenders

Servings:4 | Cooking Time: 3 Hours

Ingredients:
- 12 oz chicken fillet
- 1 tablespoon Italian seasonings
- ½ cup of water
- 1 tablespoon olive oil
- 1 teaspoon salt

Directions:
1. Cut the chicken into tenders and sprinkle with salt and Italian seasonings.
2. Then heat the oil in the skillet.
3. Add chicken tenders and cook them on high heat for 1 minute per side.
4. Then put the chicken tenders in the Crock Pot.
5. Add water and close the lid.
6. Cook the chicken for 3 hours on High.

Nutrition Info:
- Per Serving: 202 calories, 24.6g protein, 0.4g carbohydrates, 10.8g fat, 0g fiber, 75mg cholesterol, 657mg sodium, 209mg potassium.

Chicken Florentine

Servings:4 | Cooking Time: 8 Hours

Ingredients:
- 4 chicken breasts, bones and skin removed
- Salt and pepper to taste
- 2 cups parmesan cheese, divided
- ½ cup heavy cream
- 1 cup baby spinach, rinsed

Directions:
1. Place the chicken in the crockpot. Season with salt and pepper to taste.
2. Stir in half of the parmesan cheese.
3. Close the lid and cook on low for 8 hours or on high for 6 hours.
4. Halfway through the cooking time, pour in the heavy cream.
5. Continue cooking.
6. An hour after the cooking time, add in the baby spinach.
7. Cook until the spinach has wilted.

Nutrition Info:
- Calories per serving: 553; Carbohydrates: 3g; Protein: 48g; Fat: 32g; Sugar:0 g; Sodium: 952mg; Fiber: 2.6g

Cinnamon Turkey

Servings:5 | Cooking Time: 6 Hours

Ingredients:
- 1 teaspoon ground cinnamon
- 1-pound turkey fillet, chopped
- ½ teaspoon dried thyme
- 1 teaspoon salt
- ½ cup cream

Directions:
1. Mix turkey with cinnamon, salt, and thyme.
2. Transfer it in the Crock Pot.
3. Add cream and cook the meal on Low for 6 hours.

Nutrition Info:
- Per Serving: 102 calories, 19g protein, 1.1g carbohydrates, 1.8g fat, 0.2g fiber, 52mg cholesterol, 678mg sodium, 11mg potassium.

Basic Shredded Chicken

Servings:12 | Cooking Time: 8 Hours

Ingredients:
- 6 pounds chicken breasts, bones and skin removed
- 1 teaspoon salt
- ½ teaspoon black pepper
- 5 cups homemade chicken broth
- 4 tablespoons butter

Directions:
1. Place all ingredients in the CrockPot.
2. Close the lid and cook on high for 6 hours or on low for 8 hours.
3. Shred the chicken meat using two forks.
4. Return to the CrockPot and cook on high for another 30 minutes.

Nutrition Info:
- Calories per serving: 421; Carbohydrates: 0.5g; Protein: 48.1g; Fat: 25.4g; Sugar: 0g; Sodium: 802mg; Fiber: 0.1g

Rosemary Chicken In Yogurt

Servings:4 | Cooking Time: 6 Hours

Ingredients:
- 1 cup plain yogurt
- 1 tablespoon dried rosemary
- 2 tablespoons olive oil
- 1 teaspoon onion powder

- 1-pound chicken breast, skinless, boneless, chopped

Directions:
1. Rub the chicken breast with onion powder, dried rosemary, and olive oil.
2. Transfer the chicken in the Crock Pot.
3. Add plain yogurt and close the lid.
4. Cook the chicken on low for 6 hours.
5. When the meal is cooked, transfer it in the plates and top with hot yogurt mixture from the Crock Pot.

Nutrition Info:
- Per Serving: 238 calories, 27.6g protein, 5.3g carbohydrates, 10.7g fat, 0.4g fiber, 76mg cholesterol, 101mg sodium, 577mg potassium.

Bbq Pulled Chicken

Servings:3 | Cooking Time:8 Hours

Ingredients:
- 12 oz chicken breast, skinless, boneless
- ½ cup BBQ sauce
- 1 teaspoon dried rosemary
- 1 cup of water

Directions:
1. Pour water in the Crock Pot.
2. Add chicken breast and dried rosemary. Cook the chicken on High for 5 hours.
3. Then drain the water and shred the chicken with the help of the fork.
4. Add BBQ sauce, carefully mix the chicken and cook it on Low for 3 hours.

Nutrition Info:
- Per Serving: 193 calories, 24.1g protein, 15.4g carbohydrates, 3g fat, 0.4g fiber, 73mg cholesterol, 527mg sodium, 511mg potassium.

Jalapeno Chicken Wings

Servings:6 | Cooking Time: 3 Hours

Ingredients:
- 5 jalapenos, minced
- ½ cup tomato juice
- 2-pounds chicken wings, skinless
- 1 teaspoon salt
- ¼ cup of water

Directions:
1. Mix minced jalapenos with tomato juice, salt, and water.

2. Pour the liquid in the Crock Pot.
3. Add chicken wings and close the lid.
4. Cook the meal on High for 3 hours.

Nutrition Info:
- Per Serving: 294 calories, 44.1g protein, 1.6g carbohydrates, 11.3g fat, 0.4g fiber, 135mg cholesterol, 573mg sodium, 439mg potassium.

Chili Sausages

Servings:4 | Cooking Time: 3 Hours

Ingredients:
- 1-pound chicken sausages, roughly chopped
- ½ cup of water
- 1 tablespoon chili powder
- 1 teaspoon tomato paste

Directions:
1. Sprinkle the chicken sausages with chili powder and transfer in the Crock Pot.
2. Then mix water and tomato paste and pour the liquid over the chicken sausages.
3. Close the lid and cook the meal on High for 3 hours.

Nutrition Info:
- Per Serving: 221 calories, 15g protein, 8.9g carbohydrates, 12.8g fat, 1.4g fiber, 0mg cholesterol, 475mg sodium, 50mg potassium.

Turkey With Plums

Servings:5 | Cooking Time: 8 Hours

Ingredients:
- 1-pound turkey fillet, chopped
- 1 cup plums, pitted, halved
- 1 teaspoon ground cinnamon
- 1 cup of water
- 1 teaspoon ground black pepper

Directions:
1. Mix the turkey with ground cinnamon and ground black pepper.
2. Then transfer it in the Crock Pot.
3. Add water and plums.
4. Close the lid and cook the meal on Low for 8 hours.

Nutrition Info:
- Per Serving: 94 calories, 19g protein, 2.2g carbohydrates, 0.5g fat, 0.5g fiber, 47mg cholesterol, 207mg sodium, 29mg potassium.

Tender Duck Fillets

Servings:3 | Cooking Time: 8 Hours

Ingredients:
- 1 tablespoon butter
- 1 teaspoon dried rosemary
- 1 teaspoon ground nutmeg
- 9 oz duck fillet
- 1 cup of water

Directions:
1. Slice the fillet.
2. Then melt the butter in the skillet.
3. Add sliced duck fillet and roast it for 2-3 minutes per side on medium heat.
4. Transfer the roasted duck fillet and butter in the Crock Pot.
5. Add dried rosemary, ground nutmeg, and water.
6. Close the lid and cook the meal on Low for 8 hours.

Nutrition Info:
- Per Serving: 145 calories, 25.2g protein, 0.6g carbohydrates, 4.7g fat, 0.3g fiber, 10mg cholesterol, 158mg sodium, 61mg potassium.

Asian Sesame Chicken

Servings:12 | Cooking Time: 8 Hours

Ingredients:
- 12 chicken thighs, bones and skin removed
- 2 tablespoons sesame oil
- 3 tablespoons water
- 3 tablespoons soy sauce
- 1 thumb-size ginger, sliced thinly

Directions:
1. Place all ingredients in the crockpot.
2. Stir all ingredients to combine.
3. Close the lid and cook on low for 8 hours or on high for 6 hours.
4. Once cooked, garnish with toasted sesame seeds.

Nutrition Info:
- Calories per serving: 458; Carbohydrates: 1.5g; Protein: 32.2g; Fat: 35.05g; Sugar: 0g; Sodium: 426mg; Fiber: 0.4g

Breadcrumbs Mini Balls

Servings:6 | Cooking Time: 3 Hours

Ingredients:
- 1-pound ground chicken
- 1 teaspoon cayenne pepper
- 1 teaspoon salt
- ½ cup bread crumbs
- ½ cup of water

Directions:
1. Mix ground chicken with cayenne pepper, salt, and bread crumbs.
2. Then make the small balls and put them in the Crock Pot.
3. Add water and close the lid.
4. Cook the mini balls on High for 3 hours.

Nutrition Info:
- Per Serving: 180 calories, 23.1g protein, 6.7g carbohydrates, 6.1g fat, 0.5g fiber, 67mg cholesterol, 519mg sodium, 208mg potassium.

Turkey With Zucchini

Servings:4 | Cooking Time: 8 Hours

Ingredients:
- 1-pound ground turkey
- 2 red peppers cut into strips
- Salt and pepper to taste
- 2 green onions, sliced
- 1 large zucchini, sliced

Directions:
1. Place the ground turkey and red peppers in the crockpot.
2. Season with salt and pepper to taste.
3. Close the lid and cook on low for 8 hours or on high for 6 hours.
4. An hour before the cooking time is done, stir in the green onions and zucchini.
5. Cook further until the vegetables are soft.

Nutrition Info:
- Calories per serving: 195; Carbohydrates: 5.7g; Protein: 23.9g; Fat: 9.01g; Sugar: 0.4g; Sodium: 542mg; Fiber: 2.5g

Mexican Chicken In Crockpot

Servings:4 | Cooking Time: 8 Hours

Ingredients:
- 2 tablespoons butter
- 1 can diced tomatoes, undrained
- 2 cups chicken, cubed
- Salt and pepper to taste
- 1 teaspoon cumin

Directions:
1. Place all ingredients in the crockpot.
2. Mix everything to combine.
3. Close the lid and cook on low for 8 hours or on high for 5 hours.

Nutrition Info:
- Calories per serving: 594; Carbohydrates: 2.9g; Protein: 97.3 g; Fat: 21.7g; Sugar: 0.5g; Sodium: 637mg; Fiber: 0.8g

Simple Buttered Rosemary Chicken Breasts

Servings:4 | Cooking Time: 6 Hours

Ingredients:
- 5 tablespoons butter
- 4 boneless chicken breasts
- Salt and pepper to taste
- 1 tablespoon parsley
- 1 teaspoon rosemary

Directions:
1. Melt the butter in the skillet.
2. Season chicken with salt and pepper to taste. Brown all sides of the chicken for 3 minutes.
3. Transfer into the crockpot and sprinkle with parsley and rosemary.
4. Cook on low for 6 hours or on high for 5 hours.

Nutrition Info:
- Calories per serving: 459; Carbohydrates: 1.17g; Protein: 61.6g; Fat: 21.5g; Sugar: 0g; Sodium: 527mg; Fiber: 0.6g

Chicken Provolone

Servings:4 | Cooking Time: 8 Hours

Ingredients:
- 4 chicken breasts, bones and skin removed
- Salt and pepper to taste
- 8 fresh basil leaves
- 4 slices prosciutto
- 4 slices provolone cheese

Directions:
1. Sprinkle the chicken breasts with salt and pepper to taste.
2. Place in the crockpot and add the basil leaves, and prosciutto on top.
3. Arrange the provolone cheese slices on top.
4. Close the lid and cook on low for 8 hours and on high for 6 hours.

Nutrition Info:
- Calories per serving: 236; Carbohydrates: 1g; Protein: 33g; Fat: 11g; Sugar:0 g; Sodium: 435mg; Fiber:0 g

Simple Chicken And Vegetables

Servings:4 | Cooking Time: 8 Hours

Ingredients:
- 1-pound chicken breasts, bones and skin removed
- 1 sweet red bell pepper, cut into cubes
- 1 zucchini, sliced
- 1 red onion, cut into wedges
- 2/3 cup sun-dried tomatoes in vinaigrette

Directions:
1. Place all ingredients in the crockpot.
2. Give a good stir.
3. Season with salt and pepper to taste.
4. Close the lid and cook on low for 8 hours or on high for 6 hours.

Nutrition Info:
- Calories per serving: 228; Carbohydrates:4.3 g; Protein: 24g; Fat: 15g; Sugar:0 g; Sodium: 55mg; Fiber: 3.7g

Chicken With Peach And Orange Sauce

Servings: 8 | Cooking Time: 6 Hours

Ingredients:
- 6 chicken breasts, skinless and boneless
- 12 ounces orange juice
- 2 tablespoons lemon juice
- 15 ounces canned peaches and their juice
- 1 teaspoon soy sauce

Directions:
1. In your Crock Pot, mix chicken with orange juice, lemon juice, peaches and soy sauce, toss, cover and cook on Low for 6 hours.
2. Divide chicken breasts on plates, drizzle peach and orange sauce all over and serve.

Nutrition Info:
- calories 251, fat 4, fiber 6, carbs 18, protein 14

Chicken With Basil And Tomatoes

Servings:4 | Cooking Time: 8 Hours

Ingredients:
- ¾ cup balsamic vinegar
- ¼ cup fresh basil leaves
- 2 tablespoons olive oil
- 8 plum tomatoes, sliced
- 4 boneless chicken breasts, bone and skin removed

Directions:
1. Place balsamic vinegar, basil leaves, olive oil and tomatoes in a blender. Season with salt and pepper to taste. Pulse until fine.
2. Arrange the chicken pieces in the crockpot.
3. Pour over the sauce.
4. Close the lid and cook on low for 8 hours or on high for 6 hours.

Nutrition Info:
- Calories per serving: 177; Carbohydrates:4 g; Protein:24 g; Fat: 115g; Sugar: 0g; Sodium: 171mg; Fiber: 3.5g

Chicken Stuffed With Plums

Servings:6 | Cooking Time: 4 Hours

Ingredients:
- 6 chicken fillets
- 1 cup plums, pitted, sliced
- 1 cup of water
- 1 teaspoon salt
- 1 teaspoon white pepper

Directions:
1. Beat the chicken fillets gently and rub with salt and white pepper.
2. Then put the sliced plums on the chicken fillets and roll them.
3. Secure the chicken rolls with toothpicks and put in the Crock Pot.
4. Add water and close the lid.
5. Cook the meal on High for 4 hours.
6. Then remove the chicken from the Crock Pot, remove the toothpicks and transfer in the serving plates.

Nutrition Info:
- Per Serving: 283 calories, 42.4g protein, 1.6g carbohydrates, 10.9g fat, 0.2g fiber, 130mg cholesterol, 514mg sodium, 377mg potassium.

Butter Chicken

Servings:4 | Cooking Time: 4 Hours

Ingredients:
- 12 oz chicken fillet
- ½ cup butter
- 1 teaspoon garlic powder
- 1 teaspoon salt

Directions:
1. Put all ingredients in the Crock Pot.
2. Cook them on High for 4 hours.
3. Then shred the chicken and transfer in the plates.
4. Sprinkle the chicken with fragrant butter from the Crock Pot.

Nutrition Info:
- Per Serving: 367 calories, 25g protein, 0.5g carbohydrates, 29.3g fat, 0.1g fiber, 137mg cholesterol, 818mg sodium, 221mg potassium.

Chicken Vegetable Curry

Servings:6 | Cooking Time: 8 Hours

Ingredients:
- 1 tablespoon butter
- 1-pound chicken breasts, bones removed
- 1 package frozen vegetable mix
- 1 cup water
- 2 tablespoons curry powder

Directions:
1. Place all ingredients in the crockpot.
2. Stir to combine everything.
3. Close the lid and cook on low for 8 hours or on high for 6 hours.

Nutrition Info:
- Calories per serving: 273; Carbohydrates: 6.1g; Protein:21 g; Fat: 10g; Sugar: 0.1g; Sodium: 311mg; Fiber: 4g

Mediterranean Stuffed Chicken

Servings:4 | Cooking Time: 8 Hours

Ingredients:
- 4 chicken breasts, bones and skin removed
- Salt and pepper to taste
- 1 cup feta cheese, crumbled
- 1/3 cup sun-dried tomatoes, chopped
- 2 tablespoons olive oil

Directions:
1. Create a slit in the chicken breasts to thin out the meat. Season with salt and pepper to taste
2. In a mixing bowl, combine the feta cheese and sun-dried tomatoes.
3. Spoon the feta cheese mixture into the slit created into the chicken.
4. Close the slit using toothpicks.
5. Brush the chicken with olive oil.
6. Place in the crockpot and cook on high for 6 hours or on low for 8 hours.

Nutrition Info:
- Calories per serving: 332; Carbohydrates: 3g; Protein:40 g; Fat: 17g; Sugar: 0g; Sodium: 621mg; Fiber:2.4 g

Chicken In Sweet Soy Sauce

Servings:6 | Cooking Time: 6 Hours

Ingredients:
- ½ cup of soy sauce
- 2 teaspoons maple syrup
- ½ teaspoon ground cinnamon
- 6 chicken thighs, skinless, boneless
- ¼ cup of water

Directions:
1. Pour water and soy sauce in the Crock Pot.
2. Add chicken thighs, ground cinnamon, and maple syrup.
3. Close the lid and cook the meal on Low for 6 hours.

Nutrition Info:
- Per Serving: 295 calories, 43.6g protein, 3.3g carbohydrates, 10.8g fat, 0.3g fiber, 130mg cholesterol, 1324mg sodium, 406mg potassium.

Chicken With Figs

Servings:4 | Cooking Time: 7 Hours

Ingredients:
- 5 oz fresh figs, chopped
- 14 oz chicken fillet, chopped
- 1 cup of water
- 1 teaspoon peppercorns
- 1 tablespoon dried dill

Directions:
1. Put all ingredients in the Crock Pot.
2. Close the lid and cook the meal on Low for 7 hours.

Nutrition Info:
- Per Serving: 280 calories, 30.1g protein, 23.4g carbohydrates, 7.7g fat, 3.7g fiber, 88mg cholesterol, 93mg sodium, 515mg potassium.

Lemony Chicken

Servings: 6 | Cooking Time: 4 Hours

Ingredients:
- 1 whole chicken, cut into medium pieces
- Salt and black pepper to the taste
- Zest of 2 lemons
- Juice of 2 lemons
- Lemon rinds from 2 lemons

Directions:
1. Put chicken pieces in your Crock Pot, season with

salt and pepper to the taste, drizzle lemon juice, add lemon zest and lemon rinds, cover and cook on High for 4 hours.

2. Discard lemon rinds, divide chicken between plates, drizzle sauce from the Crock Pot over it and serve.

Nutrition Info:
- calories 334, fat 24, fiber 2, carbs 4.5, protein 27

Fanta Chicken

Servings:4 | Cooking Time: 4.5 Hours

Ingredients:
- 1 cup Fanta
- 1-pound chicken breast, skinless, boneless, chopped
- 1 teaspoon ground cumin
- 1 teaspoon ground nutmeg

Directions:
1. Mix chicken breast with cumin and ground nutmeg and transfer in the Crock Pot.
2. Add Fanta and close the lid.
3. Cook the meal on high for 4.5 hours.

Nutrition Info:
- Per Serving: 162 calories, 24.2g protein, 9.3g carbohydrates, 3.2g fat, 0.2g fiber, 73mg cholesterol, 68mg sodium, 431mg potassium.

Cilantro Lime Chicken

Servings:3 | Cooking Time: 8 Hours

Ingredients:
- 3 chicken breasts, bones and skin removed
- Juice from 3 limes, freshly squeezed
- 6 cloves of garlic, minced
- 1 teaspoon cumin
- ¼ cup cilantro

Directions:
1. Place all ingredients in the crockpot.
2. Give a stir to mix everything.
3. Close the lid and cook on low for 8 hours or on high for 6 hours.

Nutrition Info:
- Calories per serving: 522; Carbohydrates: 6.1g; Protein: 61.8g; Fat: 27.1g; Sugar: 2.3g; Sodium: 453mg; Fiber: 1.2g

Ground Turkey Bowl

Servings:4 | Cooking Time: 2.5 Hours

Ingredients:
- 2 tomatoes, chopped
- 10 oz ground turkey
- 1 cup Monterey Jack cheese, shredded
- ½ cup cream
- 1 teaspoon ground black pepper

Directions:
1. Put ground turkey in the Crock Pot.
2. Add cheese, cream, and ground black pepper.
3. Close the lid and cook the meal on High for 2.5 hours.
4. Then carefully mix the mixture and transfer in the serving bowls.
5. Top the ground turkey with chopped tomatoes.

Nutrition Info:
- Per Serving: 275 calories, 27.2g protein, 3.9g carbohydrates, 18.1g fat, 0.9g fiber, 103mg cholesterol, 240mg sodium, 378mg potassium.

Wine Chicken

Servings:4 | Cooking Time: 3 Hours

Ingredients:
- 1 cup red wine
- 1-pound chicken breast, skinless, boneless, chopped
- 1 anise star
- 1 teaspoon cayenne pepper
- 2 garlic cloves, crushed

Directions:
1. Pour red wine in the Crock Pot.
2. Add anise star, cayenne pepper, and garlic cloves.
3. Then add chopped chicken and close the lid.
4. Cook the meal on High for 3 hours.
5. Serve the chicken with hot wine sauce.

Nutrition Info:
- Per Serving: 182 calories, 24.2g protein, 2.4g carbohydrates, 2.9g fat, 0.2g fiber, 73mg cholesterol, 61mg sodium, 493mg potassium.

Chicken With Green Onion Sauce

Servings: 4 | Cooking Time: 4 Hrs

Ingredients:
- 2 tbsp butter, melted
- 4 green onions, chopped
- 4 chicken breast halves, skinless and boneless
- Salt and black pepper to the taste
- 8 oz. sour cream

Directions:
1. Add melted butter, chicken, and all other ingredients to the Crock Pot.
2. Put the cooker's lid on and set the cooking time to 4 hours on High settings.
3. Serve warm.

Nutrition Info:
- Per Serving: Calories: 200, Total Fat: 7g, Fiber: 2g, Total Carbs: 11g, Protein: 20g

Greece Style Chicken

Servings:6 | Cooking Time: 8 Hours

Ingredients:
- 12 oz chicken fillet, chopped
- 1 cup green olives, chopped
- 1 cup of water
- 1 tablespoon cream cheese
- ½ teaspoon dried thyme

Directions:
1. Put all ingredients in the Crock Pot.
2. Close the lid and cook the meal on Low for 8 hours.
3. Then transfer the cooked chicken in the bowls and top with olives and hot liquid from the Crock Pot.

Nutrition Info:
- Per Serving: 124 calories,16.7g protein, 0.8g carbohydrates, 5.7g fat, 0.3g fiber, 52mg cholesterol, 167mg sodium, 142mg potassium.

Easy Chicken Continental

Servings:2 | Cooking Time: 7 Hours

Ingredients:
- 2 oz dried beef
- 8 oz chicken breast, skinless, boneless, chopped
- ½ cup cream
- ½ can onion soup
- 1 tablespoon cornstarch

Directions:
1. Put 1 oz of the dried beef in the Crock Pot in one layer.
2. Then add chicken breast and top it with remaining dried beef.
3. After this, mix cream cheese, onion, and cornstarch. Whisk the mixture and pour it over the chicken and dried beef.
4. Cook the meal on Low for 7 hours.

Nutrition Info:
- Per Serving: 270 calories, 35.4g protein, 10.5g carbohydrates, 9g fat, 0.6g fiber, 109mg cholesterol, 737mg sodium, 598mg potassium.

Chicken Sausages In Jam

Servings:4 | Cooking Time: 6 Hours

Ingredients:
- ½ cup of strawberry jam
- ½ cup of water
- 1-pound chicken breast, skinless, boneless, chopped
- 1 teaspoon white pepper

Directions:
1. Sprinkle the chicken meat with white pepper and put it in the Crock Pot.
2. Then mix jam with water and pour the liquid over the chicken.
3. Close the lid and cook it on Low for 6 hours.

Nutrition Info:
- Per Serving: 282 calories, 24.1g protein, 37.5g carbohydrates, 2.9g fat, 0.1g fiber, 73mg cholesterol, 59mg sodium, 427mg potassium.

Garlic Pulled Chicken

Servings:4 | Cooking Time: 4 Hours

Ingredients:
- 1-pound chicken breast, skinless, boneless
- 1 tablespoon minced garlic
- 2 cups of water
- ½ cup plain yogurt

Directions:
1. Put the chicken breast in the Crock Pot.
2. Add minced garlic and water.
3. Close the lid and cook the chicken on High for 4 hours.
4. Then drain water and shred the chicken breast.
5. Add plain yogurt and stir the pulled chicken well.

Nutrition Info:
- Per Serving: 154 calories, 25.9g protein, 2.9g carbohydrates, 3.2g fat, 0g fiber, 74mg cholesterol, 83mg sodium, 501mg potassium.

Vinegar Chicken Wings

Servings:8 | Cooking Time: 3 Hours

Ingredients:
- ½ cup apple cider vinegar
- 1 teaspoon garlic powder
- 1 teaspoon smoked paprika
- ½ cup plain yogurt
- 3-pounds chicken wings

Directions:
1. Mix plain yogurt with smoked paprika, garlic powder, and apple cider vinegar.
2. Pour the liquid in the Crock Pot.
3. Add chicken wings and close the lid.
4. Cook the meal on High for 3 hours.

Nutrition Info:
- Per Serving: 339 calories, 50.2g protein, 1.6g carbohydrates, 12.8g fat, 0.1g fiber, 152mg cholesterol, 158mg sodium, 470mg potassium.

Lemon Parsley Chicken

Servings:4 | Cooking Time: 8 Hours

Ingredients:
- 2 tablespoons butter, melted
- 1-pound chicken breasts, bones removed
- Salt and pepper to taste
- 1 lemon, sliced thinly
- ½ cup parsley, chopped

Directions:
1. Line the bottom of the crockpot with foil.
2. Grease the foil with melted butter.
3. Season the chicken breasts with salt and pepper to taste.
4. Arrange on the foil and place lemon slices on top.
5. Sprinkle with chopped parsley.
6. Cook on low for 8 hours or on high for 6 hours

Nutrition Info:
- Calories per serving: 303; Carbohydrates: 3.1g; Protein: 34.5g; Fat: 14g; Sugar: 0.7g; Sodium: 430mg; Fiber: 1g

Chicken, Peppers And Onions

Servings:4 | Cooking Time: 8 Hours

Ingredients:
- 1 tablespoon olive oil
- ½ cup shallots, peeled
- 1-pound boneless chicken breasts, sliced
- ½ cup green and red peppers, diced
- Salt and pepper to taste

Directions:
1. Heat oil in a skillet over medium flame.
2. Sauté the shallots until fragrant and translucent. Allow to cook so that the outer edges of the shallots turn slightly brown.
3. Transfer into the crockpot.
4. Add the chicken breasts and the peppers.
5. Season with salt and pepper to taste.
6. Add a few tablespoons of water.
7. Close the lid and cook on low for 8 hours or on high for 6 hours.

Nutrition Info:
- Calories per serving: 179; Carbohydrates: 3.05g; Protein:26.1 g; Fat: 10.4g; Sugar: 0g; Sodium: 538mg; Fiber:2.4 g

Chicken And Green Onion Sauce

Servings: 4 | Cooking Time: 4 Hours

Ingredients:
- 2 tablespoons butter, melted
- 4 green onions, chopped
- 4 chicken breast halves, skinless and boneless
- Salt and black pepper to the taste
- 8 ounces sour cream

Directions:
1. In your Crock Pot, mix chicken with melted butter, green onion, salt, pepper and sour cream, cover and cook on High for 4 hours.
2. Divide chicken between plates, drizzle green onions sauce all over and serve.

Nutrition Info:
- calories 200, fat 7, fiber 2, carbs 11, protein 20

Stuffed Whole Chicken

Servings:10 | Cooking Time: 6 Hours

Ingredients:
- 3-pound whole chicken
- 1 tablespoon taco seasonings
- 1 cup apples, chopped
- 1 tablespoon olive oil
- 2 cups of water

Directions:
1. Fill the chicken with apples.
2. Then rub the chicken with taco seasonings and brush with olive oil.
3. Place it in the Crock Pot. Add water.
4. Cook the chicken on High for 6 hours.
5. When the chicken is cooked, chop it into servings and serve with cooked apples.

Nutrition Info:
- Per Serving: 285 calories, 39.4g protein, 3.7g carbohydrates, 11.5g fat, 0.5g fiber, 121mg cholesterol, 182mg sodium, 355mg potassium.

Chapter 6 Fish & Seafood Recipes

Chapter 6 Fish & Seafood Recipes

Curry Shrimps

Servings:4 | Cooking Time: 45 Minutes

Ingredients:
- 16 oz shrimps, peeled
- 1 teaspoon curry paste
- ½ cup fish stock

Directions:
1. Mix the curry paste with fish stock and pour it in the Crock Pot.
2. Add shrimps and cook them on High for 45 minutes.

Nutrition Info:
- Per Serving: 148 calories, 26.6g protein, 2.1g carbohydrates, 2.9g fat, 0g fiber, 239mg cholesterol, 322mg sodium, 234mg potassium

Smelt In Avocado Oil

Servings:4 | Cooking Time: 4 Hours

Ingredients:
- 12 oz smelt fillet
- 1 teaspoon chili powder
- ¼ teaspoon ground turmeric
- ½ teaspoon smoked paprika
- 4 tablespoons avocado oil

Directions:
1. Cut the smelt fillet into 4 servings.
2. Then sprinkle every fish fillet with chili powder, ground turmeric, and smoked paprika.
3. Put the fish in the Crock Pot.
4. Add avocado oil and close the lid.
5. Cook the fish on Low for 4 hours.

Nutrition Info:
- Per Serving: 89 calories, 13.1g protein, 1.4g carbohydrates, 3.5g fat, 1g fiber, 112mg cholesterol, 52mg sodium, 66mg potassium

Curry Clams

Servings:4 | Cooking Time: 1.5 Hour

Ingredients:
- 1-pound clams
- 1 teaspoon curry paste
- ¼ cup of coconut milk
- 1 cup of water

Directions:
1. Mix coconut milk with curry paste and water and pour it in the Crock Pot.
2. Add clams and close the lid.
3. Cook the meal on High for 1.5 hours or until the clams are opened.

Nutrition Info:
- Per Serving: 97 calories, 1.1g protein, 13.6g carbohydrates, 4.5g fat, 0.8g fiber, 0mg cholesterol, 415mg sodium, 141mg potassium.

Turmeric Mackerel

Servings:4 | Cooking Time: 2.5 Hours

Ingredients:
- 1-pound mackerel fillet
- 1 tablespoon ground turmeric
- ½ teaspoon salt
- ¼ teaspoon chili powder
- ½ cup of water

Directions:
1. Rub the mackerel fillet with ground turmeric and chili powder.
2. Then put it in the Crock Pot.
3. Add water and salt.
4. Close the lid and cook the fish on High for 2.5 hours.

Nutrition Info:
- Per Serving: 304 calories, 27.2g protein, 1.2g carbohydrates, 20.4g fat, 0.4g fiber, 58mg cholesterol, 388mg sodium, 501mg potassium

Mackerel Bites

Servings:4 | Cooking Time: 3 Hours

Ingredients:
- 1-pound mackerel fillet, chopped
- 1 tablespoon avocado oil
- ½ teaspoon ground paprika
- ½ teaspoon ground turmeric
- 1/3 cup water

Directions:
1. In the shallow bowl mix ground paprika with ground turmeric.
2. Then sprinkle the mackerel fillet with a spice mixture.
3. Heat the avocado oil in the skillet well.
4. Add fish and roast it for 1 minute per side on high heat.
5. Pour water in the Crock Pot.
6. Add fish and close the lid.
7. Cook the mackerel bites on High for 3 hours.

Nutrition Info:
- Per Serving: 304 calories, 27.2g protein, 0.5g carbohydrates, 20.7g fat, 0.3g fiber, 85mg cholesterol, 95mg sodium, 479mg potassium

Basil Octopus

Servings:3 | Cooking Time: 4 Hours

Ingredients:
- 12 oz octopus, chopped
- 1 orange, chopped
- 1 teaspoon dried basil
- ½ cup of water
- 1 teaspoon butter

Directions:
1. Put all ingredients in the Crock Pot.
2. Close the lid and cook the octopus on Low for 4 hours or until it is soft.

Nutrition Info:
- Per Serving: 226 calories, 34.4g protein, 12.2g carbohydrates, 3.7g fat, 1.5g fiber, 112mg cholesterol, 532mg sodium, 827mg potassium

Lemony Shrimps In Hoisin Sauce

Servings:4 | Cooking Time: 2 Hours

Ingredients:
- 1/3 cup hoisin sauce
- ½ cup lemon juice, freshly squeezed
- 1 ½ pounds shrimps, shelled and deveined
- Salt and pepper to taste
- 2 tablespoon cilantro leaves, chopped

Directions:
1. Into the crockpot, place the hoisin sauce, lemon juice, and shrimps.
2. Season with salt and pepper to taste.
3. Mix to incorporate all ingredients.
4. Close the lid and cook on high for 30 minutes or on low for 2 hours.
5. Garnish with cilantro leaves.

Nutrition Info:
- Calories per serving: 228; Carbohydrates: 6.3g; Protein: 35.8g; Fat: 3.2g; Sugar: 0g; Sodium: 482mg; Fiber: 4.8g

Mustard Cod

Servings:4 | Cooking Time: 3 Hours

Ingredients:
- 4 cod fillets
- 4 teaspoons mustard
- 2 tablespoons sesame oil
- ¼ cup of water

Directions:
1. Mix mustard with sesame oil.
2. Then brush the cod fillets with mustard mixture and transfer in the Crock Pot.
3. Add water and cook the fish on low for 3 hours.

Nutrition Info:
- Per Serving: 166 calories, 20.8g protein, 1.2g carbohydrates, 8.8g fat, 0.5g fiber, 55mg cholesterol, 71mg sodium, 23mg potassium

Prosciutto-wrapped Scallops

Servings:4 | Cooking Time: 3 Hours

Ingredients:
- 12 large scallops, rinsed and patted dry
- Salt and pepper to taste
- 1 ¼ ounces prosciutto, cut into 12 long strips

- 1 tablespoon extra-virgin olive oil
- 1 tablespoon lemon juice

Directions:

1. Sprinkle individual scallops with salt and pepper to taste.
2. Wrap a prosciutto around the scallops. Set aside.
3. Add oil in crockpot and arrange on top the bacon-wrapped scallops.
4. Pour over the lemon juice.
5. Cook on low for 1 hour or on high for 3 hours.
6. Halfway through the cooking time, flip the scallops.
7. Continue cooking until scallops are done.

Nutrition Info:

- Calories per serving: 113; Carbohydrates: 5g; Protein: 15.9g; Fat:8 g; Sugar:0 g; Sodium: 424mg; Fiber: 3.2g

Vegan Milk Clams

Servings:4 | Cooking Time: 3 Hours

Ingredients:

- 1 cup organic almond milk
- 1 teaspoon dried parsley
- 1 teaspoon dried dill
- ½ teaspoon salt
- 1-pound clams

Directions:

1. Put all ingredients in the Crock Pot and gently mix.
2. Close the lid and cook the clams on Low for 3 hours.

Nutrition Info:

- Per Serving: 70 calories, 1g protein, 14.6g carbohydrates, 0.9g fat, 0.5g fiber, 0mg cholesterol, 737mg sodium, 111mg potassium

Sweet And Sour Shrimps

Servings:2 | Cooking Time: 50 Minutes

Ingredients:

- 8 oz shrimps, peeled
- ½ cup of water
- 2 tablespoons lemon juice
- 1 tablespoon maple syrup

Directions:

1. Pour water in the Crock Pot.
2. Add shrimps and cook them on High for 50 minutes.

3. Then drain water and ass lemon juice and maple syrup.
4. Carefully stir the shrimps and transfer them in the serving bowls.

Nutrition Info:

- Per Serving: 165 calories, 26g protein, 8.8g carbohydrates, 2.1g fat, 0.1g fiber, 239mg cholesterol, 282mg sodium, 232mg potassium.

Braised Salmon

Servings:4 | Cooking Time: 1 Hour

Ingredients:

- 1 cup of water
- 2-pound salmon fillet
- 1 teaspoon salt
- 1 teaspoon ground black pepper

Directions:

1. Put all ingredients in the Crock Pot and close the lid.
2. Cook the salmon on High for 1 hour.

Nutrition Info:

- Per Serving: 301 calories, 44.1g protein, 0.3g carbohydrates, 14g fat, 0.1g fiber, 100mg cholesterol, 683mg sodium, 878mg potassium.

Apple Cider Vinegar Sardines

Servings:4 | Cooking Time: 4.5 Hours

Ingredients:

- 14 oz sardines
- 1 tablespoon butter
- ¼ cup apple cider vinegar
- ½ teaspoon cayenne pepper
- 4 tablespoons coconut cream

Directions:

1. Put sardines in the Crock Pot.
2. Add butter, apple cider vinegar, cayenne pepper, and coconut cream.
3. Close the lid and cook the meal on Low for 4.5 hours.

Nutrition Info:

- Per Serving: 270 calories, 24.8g protein, 1.1g carbohydrates, 17.9g fat, 0.4g fiber, 149mg cholesterol,525mg sodium, 450mg potassium

Buttered Bacon And Scallops

Servings:4 | Cooking Time: 2 Hours

Ingredients:
- 1 tablespoon butter
- 2 cloves of garlic, chopped
- 24 scallops, rinsed and patted dry
- Salt and pepper to taste
- 1 cup bacon, chopped

Directions:

1. In a skillet, heat the butter and sauté the garlic until fragrant and lightly browned.
2. Transfer to a crockpot and add the scallops.
3. Season with salt and pepper to taste.
4. Close the lid and cook on high for 45 minutes or on low for 2 hours.
5. Meanwhile, cook the bacon until the fat has rendered and crispy.
6. Sprinkle the cooked scallops with crispy bacon.

Nutrition Info:
- Calories per serving: 261; Carbohydrates:4.9 g; Protein:24.7 g; Fat:14.3 g; Sugar: 1.3g; Sodium: 425mg; Fiber: 3g

Almond-crusted Tilapia

Servings:4 | Cooking Time: 4 Hours

Ingredients:
- 2 tablespoons olive oil
- 1 cup chopped almonds
- ¼ cup ground flaxseed
- 4 tilapia fillets
- Salt and pepper to taste

Directions:

1. Line the bottom of the crockpot with a foil.
2. Grease the foil with the olive oil.
3. In a mixing bowl, combine the almonds and flaxseed.
4. Season the tilapia with salt and pepper to taste.
5. Dredge the tilapia fillets with the almond and flaxseed mixture.
6. Place neatly in the foil-lined crockpot.
7. Close the lid and cook on high for 2 hours and on low for 4 hours.

Nutrition Info:
- Calories per serving: 233; Carbohydrates: 4.6g; Protein: 25.5g; Fat: 13.3g; Sugar: 0.4g; Sodium: 342mg; Fiber: 1.9g

Salmon With Green Peppercorn Sauce

Servings:4 | Cooking Time: 3 Hours

Ingredients:
- 1 ¼ pounds salmon fillets, skin removed and cut into 4 portions
- Salt and pepper to taste
- 4 teaspoons unsalted butter
- ¼ cup lemon juice
- 1 teaspoon green peppercorns in vinegar

Directions:

1. Sprinkle the salmon fillets with salt and pepper to taste.
2. In a skillet, heat the butter and sear the salmon fillets for 2 minutes on each side.
3. Transfer in the crockpot and pour the lemon juice and green peppercorns.
4. Adjust the seasoning by adding in more salt or pepper depending on your taste.
5. Close the lid and cook on high for 1 hour or on low for 3 hours.

Nutrition Info:
- Calories per serving: 255; Carbohydrates: 2.3g; Protein: 37.4g; Fat: 13.5g; Sugar: 0g; Sodium: 352mg; Fiber: 1.5g

Salmon Stew

Servings: 6 | Cooking Time: 5 Hours 15 Minutes

Ingredients:
- 2 tablespoons butter
- 2 pounds salmon fillet, cubed
- 2 medium onions, chopped
- Salt and black pepper, to taste
- 2 cups homemade fish broth

Directions:

1. Put all the ingredients in the one pot crock pot and thoroughly mix.
2. Cover and cook on LOW for about 5 hours.
3. Dish out and serve hot.

Nutrition Info:
- Calories: 293 Fat: 8.7g Carbohydrates: 16.3g

Thyme And Sesame Halibut

Servings:2 | Cooking Time: 4 Hours

Ingredients:
- 1 tablespoon lemon juice
- 1 teaspoon thyme
- Salt and pepper to taste
- 8 ounces halibut or mahi-mahi, cut into 2 portions
- 1 tablespoons sesame seeds, toasted

Directions:
1. Line the bottom of the crockpot with a foil.
2. Mix lemon juice, thyme, salt and pepper in a shallow dish.
3. Place the fish and allow to marinate for 2 hours in the fish.
4. Sprinkle the fish with toasted sesame seeds.
5. Arrange the fish in the foil-lined crockpot.
6. Close the lid and cook on high for 2 hours or on low for 4 hours.

Nutrition Info:
- Calories per serving: 238; Carbohydrates: 3.9g; Protein: 23.1g; Fat: 14.9g; Sugar: 0.5g; Sodium:313 mg; Fiber:1.6 g

Miso Cod

Servings:4 | Cooking Time: 4 Hours

Ingredients:
- 1-pound cod fillet, sliced
- 1 teaspoon miso paste
- ½ teaspoon ground ginger
- 2 cups chicken stock
- ½ teaspoon ground nutmeg

Directions:
1. In the mixing bowl mix chicken stock, ground nutmeg, ground ginger, and miso paste.
2. Then pour the liquid in the Crock Pot.
3. Add cod fillet and close the lid.
4. Cook the fish on Low for 4 hours.

Nutrition Info:
- Per Serving: 101 calories, 20.8g protein, 1.1g carbohydrates, 1.5g fat, 0.2g fiber, 56mg cholesterol, 506mg sodium, 14mg potassium.

Butter Crab Legs

Servings:4 | Cooking Time: 45 Minutes

Ingredients:
- 15 oz king crab legs
- 1 tablespoon butter
- 1 cup of water
- 1 teaspoon dried basil

Directions:
1. Put the crab legs in the Crock Pot.
2. Add basil and water and cook them on High for 45 minutes.

Nutrition Info:
- Per Serving: 133 calories, 20.4g protein, 0g carbohydrates, 4.5g fat, 0g fiber, 67mg cholesterol, 1161mg sodium, 2mg potassium

Bigeye Jack Saute

Servings:4 | Cooking Time: 6 Hours

Ingredients:
- 7 oz (bigeye jack) tuna fillet, chopped
- 1 cup tomato, chopped
- 1 teaspoon ground black pepper
- 1 jalapeno pepper, chopped
- ½ cup chicken stock

Directions:
1. Put all ingredients in the Crock Pot and close the lid.
2. Cook the saute on Low for 6 hours.

Nutrition Info:
- Per Serving: 192 calories, 11g protein, 2.4g carbohydrates, 15.6g fat, 0.8g fiber, 0mg cholesterol, 98mg sodium, 123mg potassium

Spicy Basil Shrimp

Servings:4 | Cooking Time: 2 Hours

Ingredients:
- 1-pound raw shrimp, shelled and deveined
- Salt and pepper to taste
- 1 tablespoon butter
- ¼ cup packed fresh basil leaves
- ¼ teaspoon cayenne pepper

Directions:
1. Add all ingredients in the crockpot.
2. Give a stir.

3. Close the lid and cook on high for 30 minutes or on low for 2 hours.

Nutrition Info:
- Calories per serving: 144; Carbohydrates: 1.4g; Protein: 23.4g; Fat: 6.2g; Sugar: 0g; Sodium: 126mg; Fiber:0.5 g

Parsley Salmon

Servings: 6 | Cooking Time: 5 Hours 30 Minutes

Ingredients:
- ¼ teaspoon ginger powder
- 2 tablespoons olive oil
- 24-ounce salmon fillets
- Salt and black pepper, to taste
- 3 tablespoons fresh parsley, minced

Directions:
1. Mix together all the ingredients except salmon fillets in a bowl.
2. Marinate salmon fillets in this mixture for about 1 hour.
3. Transfer the marinated salmon fillets into the crock pot and cover the lid.
4. Cook on LOW for about 5 hours and dish out to serve hot.

Nutrition Info:
- Calories: 191 Fat: 11.7 g Carbohydrates: 0.2 g

Taco Mackerel

Servings:4 | Cooking Time: 1.5 Hours

Ingredients:
- 12 oz mackerel fillets
- 1 tablespoon taco seasonings
- 2 tablespoons coconut oil
- 3 tablespoons water

Directions:
1. Melt the coconut oil in the skillet and heat it well.
2. Meanwhile, rub the mackerel fillets with taco seasonings.
3. Put the fish in the hot coconut oil.
4. Roast it for 2 minutes per side.
5. Then put the roasted fish in the Crock Pot.
6. Add water and cook it on High for 1.5 hours.

Nutrition Info:
- Per Serving: 289 calories, 20.3g protein, 1g carbohydrates, 22g fat, 0g fiber, 64mg cholesterol, 176mg sodium, 341mg potassium

Scallops With Sour Cream And Dill

Servings:4 | Cooking Time: 2 Hours

Ingredients:
- 1 ¼ pounds scallops
- Salt and pepper to taste
- 3 teaspoons butter
- ¼ cup sour cream
- 1 tablespoon fresh dill

Directions:
1. Add all ingredients into the crockpot.
2. Give a good stir to combine everything.
3. Close the lid and cook on high for 30 minutes or on low for 2 hours.

Nutrition Info:
- Calories per serving: 152; Carbohydrates: 4.3g; Protein: 18.2g; Fat: 5.7g; Sugar: 0.5g; Sodium: 231mg; Fiber: 2.3g

Butter Tilapia

Servings:4 | Cooking Time: 6 Hours

Ingredients:
- 4 tilapia fillets
- ½ cup butter
- 1 teaspoon dried dill
- ½ teaspoon ground black pepper

Directions:
1. Sprinkle the tilapia fillets with dried dill and ground black pepper. Put them in the Crock Pot.
2. Add butter.
3. Cook the tilapia on Low for 6 hours.

Nutrition Info:
- Per Serving: 298 calories, 21.3g protein, 0.3g carbohydrates, 24.1g fat, 0.1g fiber, 116mg cholesterol, 204mg sodium, 18mg potassium

Crab Bake

Servings:4 | Cooking Time: 1.5 Hours

Ingredients:
- 1 cup Cheddar cheese, shredded
- 1-pound crab meat, cooked, chopped
- 1 teaspoon white pepper
- 1 teaspoon dried cilantro
- 1 cup cream

Directions:

1. Put crab meat in the Crock Pot and flatten it in one layer.
2. Sprinkle it with white pepper and dried cilantro.
3. After this, pour the cream and sprinkle the crab meat with Cheddar cheese.
4. Close the lid and cook the meal on High for 1.5 hours.

Nutrition Info:
- Per Serving: 255 calories, 21.8g protein, 4.6g carbohydrates, 14.7g fat, 0.1g fiber, 102mg cholesterol, 904mg sodium, 57mg potassium.

Garlic Perch

Servings:4 | Cooking Time: 4 Hours

Ingredients:
- 1-pound perch
- 1 teaspoon minced garlic
- 1 tablespoon butter, softened
- 1 tablespoon fish sauce
- ½ cup of water

Directions:
1. In the shallow bowl mix minced garlic, butter, and fish sauce.
2. Rub the perch with a garlic butter mixture and arrange it in the Crock Pot.
3. Add remaining garlic butter mixture and water.
4. Cook the fish on high for 4 hours.

Nutrition Info:
- Per Serving: 161 calories, 28.5g protein, 0.4g carbohydrates, 4.2g fat, 0g fiber, 138mg cholesterol, 458mg sodium, 407mg potassium.

Soy Sauce Scallops

Servings:4 | Cooking Time: 30 Minutes

Ingredients:
- ¼ cup of soy sauce
- 1 tablespoon butter
- ½ teaspoon white pepper
- 1-pound scallops

Directions:
1. Pour soy sauce in the Crock Pot.
2. Add butter and white pepper.
3. After this, add scallops and close the lid.
4. Cook them on High for 30 minutes.

Nutrition Info:

- Per Serving: 134 calories, 20.1g protein, 4.1g carbohydrates, 3.8g fat, 0.2g fiber, 45mg cholesterol, 1102mg sodium, 404mg potassium

Cod With Asparagus

Servings: 4 | Cooking Time: 2 Hrs

Ingredients:
- 4 cod fillets, boneless
- 1 bunch asparagus
- 12 tbsp lemon juice
- Salt and black pepper to the taste
- 2 tbsp olive oil

Directions:
1. Place the cod fillets in separate foil sheets.
2. Top the fish with asparagus spears, lemon pepper, oil, and lemon juice.
3. Wrap the fish with its foil sheet then place them in Crock Pot.
4. Put the cooker's lid on and set the cooking time to 2 hours on High settings.
5. Unwrap the fish and serve warm.

Nutrition Info:
- Per Serving: Calories 202, Total Fat 3g, Fiber 6g, Total Carbs 7g, Protein 3g

Coconut Curry Cod

Servings:2 | Cooking Time: 2.5 Hours

Ingredients:
- 2 cod fillets
- ½ teaspoon curry paste
- 1/3 cup coconut milk
- 1 teaspoon sunflower oil

Directions:
1. Mix coconut milk with curry paste, add sunflower oil, and transfer the liquid in the Crock Pot.
2. Add cod fillets.
3. Cook the meal on High for 2.5 hours.

Nutrition Info:
- Per Serving: 211 calories, 21g protein, 2.6g carbohydrates, 13.6g fat, 0.9g fiber, 55mg cholesterol, 76mg sodium, 105mg potassium

Crockpot Greek Snapper

Servings:8 | Cooking Time: 4 Hours

Ingredients:
- 3 tablespoons olive oil
- 12 snapper fillets
- 1 tablespoon Greek seasoning
- 24 lemon slices
- Salt and pepper to taste

Directions:
1. Line the bottom of the crockpot with foil.
2. Grease the foil with olive oil
3. Season the snapper fillets with Greek seasoning, salt, and pepper.
4. Arrange lemon slices on top.
5. Close the lid and cook on high for 2 hours and on low for 4 hours.

Nutrition Info:
- Calories per serving: 409; Carbohydrates: 4.3g; Protein:67 g; Fat: 15.3g; Sugar: 0g; Sodium: 246mg; Fiber: 1.8g

Butter Salmon

Servings:2 | Cooking Time: 1.5 Hours

Ingredients:
- 8 oz salmon fillet
- 3 tablespoons butter
- 1 teaspoon dried sage
- ¼ cup of water

Directions:
1. Churn butter with sage and preheat the mixture until liquid.
2. Then cut the salmon fillets into 2 servings and put in the Crock Pot.
3. Add water and melted butter mixture.
4. Close the lid and cook the salmon on High for 1.5 hours.

Nutrition Info:
- Per Serving: 304 calories, 22.2g protein, 0.2g carbohydrates, 24.3g fat, 0.1g fiber, 96mg cholesterol, 174mg sodium, 444mg potassium.

Rosemary Seabass

Servings:3 | Cooking Time: 4 Hours

Ingredients:
- 3 seabass fillets
- 1 teaspoon dried rosemary
- 1 carrot, grated
- 2 teaspoons sesame oil
- ½ cup of water

Directions:
1. Rub the seabass fillets with dried rosemary and sesame oil.
2. Then place them in the Crock Pot in one layer.
3. Top the fillets with grated carrot.
4. Add water and close the lid.
5. Cook the fish on low for 4 hours.

Nutrition Info:
- Per Serving: 271 calories, 26.3g protein, 2.3g carbohydrates, 17.2g fat, 1.6g fiber, 0mg cholesterol, 16mg sodium, 69mg potassium.

Shrimps And Carrot Saute

Servings:4 | Cooking Time: 6 Hours

Ingredients:
- 1 cup carrot, diced
- 1-pound shrimps, peeled
- 1 cup tomatoes, chopped
- ½ cup of water
- 1 teaspoon fennel seeds

Directions:
1. Put all ingredients in the Crock Pot.
2. Gently mix the mixture and close the lid.
3. Cook the saute on Low for 6 hours.

Nutrition Info:
- Per Serving: 156 calories, 26.5g protein, 6.4g carbohydrates, 2.1g fat, 1.4g fiber, 239mg cholesterol, 299mg sodium, 395mg potassium

Chili Salmon

Servings:4 | Cooking Time: 5 Hours

Ingredients:
- 1-pound salmon fillet, chopped
- 3 oz chili, chopped, canned
- ½ cup of water
- ½ teaspoon salt

Directions:

1. Place all ingredients in the Crock Pot and close the lid.
2. Cook the meal on Low for 5 hours.

Nutrition Info:

• Per Serving: 174 calories, 23.2g protein, 2.5g carbohydrates,8.2g fat, 0.9g fiber, 54mg cholesterol, 453mg sodium, 513mg potassium.

Express Shrimps And Sausage Jambalaya Stew

Servings:4 | Cooking Time: 3 Hours

Ingredients:

• 1 teaspoon canola oil
• 8 ounces andouille sausage, cut into slices
• 1 16-ounce bag frozen bell pepper and onion mix
• 1 can chicken broth
• 8 ounces shrimps, shelled and deveined

Directions:

1. In a skillet, heat the oil and sauté the sausages until the sausages have rendered their fat. Set aside.
2. Pour the vegetable mix into the crockpot.
3. Add in the sausages and pour the chicken broth.
4. Stir in the shrimps last.
5. Cook on low for 1 hour or on low for 3 hours.

Nutrition Info:

• Calories per serving: 316; Carbohydrates: 6.3; Protein: 32.1g; Fat: 25.6g; Sugar:0.2 g; Sodium: 425mg; Fiber: 3.2g

Apricot And Halibut Saute

Servings:2 | Cooking Time: 5 Hours

Ingredients:

• 6 oz halibut fillet, chopped
• ½ cup apricots, pitted, chopped
• ½ cup of water
• 1 tablespoon soy sauce
• 1 teaspoon ground cumin

Directions:

1. Put all ingredients in the Crock Pot.
2. Close the lid and cook the fish sauté on Low for 5 hours.

Nutrition Info:

• Per Serving: 407 calories, 28.7g protein, 5.3g carbohydrates, 28.7g fat, 0.9g fiber, 94mg cholesterol,

619mg sodium, 684mg potassium.

Rosemary Sole

Servings:2 | Cooking Time: 2 Hours

Ingredients:

• 8 oz sole fillet
• 1 tablespoon dried rosemary
• 1 tablespoon avocado oil
• 1 tablespoon apple cider vinegar
• 5 tablespoons water

Directions:

1. Pour water in the Crock Pot.
2. Then rub the sole fillet with dried rosemary and sprinkle with avocado oil and apple cider vinegar.
3. Put the fish fillet in the Crock Pot and cook it on High for 2 hours.

Nutrition Info:

• Per Serving: 149 calories, 27.6g protein, 1.5g carbohydrates, 2.9g fat, 1g fiber, 77mg cholesterol, 122mg sodium, 434mg potassium.

Sriracha Cod

Servings:4 | Cooking Time: 6 Hours

Ingredients:

• 4 cod fillets
• 2 tablespoons sriracha
• 1 tablespoon olive oil
• 1 teaspoon tomato paste
• ½ cup of water

Directions:

1. Sprinkle the cod fillets with sriracha, olive oil, and tomato paste.
2. Put the fish in the Crock Pot and add water.
3. Cook it on Low for 6 hours.

Nutrition Info:

• Per Serving: 129 calories, 20.1g protein, 1.8g carbohydrates, 4.5g fat, 0.1g fiber, 55mg cholesterol, 125mg sodium, 14mg potassium.

Creamy Pangasius

Servings:4 | Cooking Time: 2.5 Hours

Ingredients:
- 4 pangasius fillets
- ½ cup cream
- 1 teaspoon cornflour
- 1 tablespoon fish sauce
- 1 teaspoon ground nutmeg

Directions:
1. Coat the fish fillets in the cornflour and sprinkle with ground nutmeg.
2. Put the fish in the Crock Pot.
3. Add cream and fish sauce.
4. Close the lid and cook the meal on High for 2.5 hours.

Nutrition Info:
- Per Serving: 106 calories, 15.5g protein, 1.8g carbohydrates, 4.9g fat, 0.2g fiber, 26mg cholesterol, 617mg sodium, 28mg potassium

Braised Lobster

Servings:4 | Cooking Time: 3 Hours

Ingredients:
- 2-pound lobster, cleaned
- 1 cup of water
- 1 teaspoon Italian seasonings

Directions:
1. Put all ingredients in the Crock Pot.
2. Close the lid and cook the lobster in High for 3 hours.
3. Remove the lobster from the Crock Pot and cool it till room temperature

Nutrition Info:
- Per Serving: 206 calories, 43.1g protein, 0.1g carbohydrates, 2.2g fat, 0g fiber, 332mg cholesterol, 1104mg sodium, 524mg potassium.

Spicy Curried Shrimps

Servings:4 | Cooking Time: 2 Hours

Ingredients:
- 1 ½ pounds shrimp, shelled and deveined
- 1 tablespoon ghee or butter, melted
- 1 tablespoon curry powder
- 1 teaspoon cayenne pepper

- Salt and pepper to taste

Directions:
1. Place all ingredients in the crockpot.
2. Give a stir to incorporate everything.
3. Close the lid and allow to cook on low for 2 hours or on high for 30 minutes.

Nutrition Info:
- Calories per serving: 207; Carbohydrates:2.2 g; Protein: 35.2g; Fat: 10.5g; Sugar: 0g; Sodium: 325mg; Fiber: 1.6g

Easy Salmon And Kimchi Sauce

Servings: 4 | Cooking Time: 2 Hours

Ingredients:
- 2 tablespoons butter, soft
- 1 and ¼ pound salmon fillet
- 2 ounces Kimchi, finely chopped
- Salt and black pepper to the taste

Directions:
1. In your food processor, mix butter with Kimchi, blend well, rub salmon with salt, pepper and Kimchi mix, place in your Crock Pot, cover and cook on High for 2 hours.
2. Divide between plates and serve with a side salad.

Nutrition Info:
- calories 270, fat 12, fiber 5, carbs 13, protein 21

Sweet And Mustard Tilapia

Servings:4 | Cooking Time: 4.5 Hours

Ingredients:
- 16 oz tilapia fillets
- 1 teaspoon brown sugar
- 2 tablespoons mustard
- 1 tablespoon sesame oil
- ¼ cup of water

Directions:
1. Mix brown sugar with mustard and sesame oil.
2. Carefully rub the tilapia fillets with mustard mixture and transfer them in the Crock Pot.
3. Add water.
4. Cook the tilapia on Low for 5 hours.

Nutrition Info:
- Per Serving: 153 calories, 22.5g protein, 2.7g carbohydrates, 6g fat, 0.8g fiber, 55mg cholesterol, 41mg sodium, 39mg potassium

Chili-rubbed Tilapia

Servings:4 | Cooking Time: 4 Hours

Ingredients:
- 2 tablespoons chili powder
- ½ teaspoon garlic powder
- 1-pound tilapia
- 2 tablespoons lemon juice
- 2 tablespoons olive oil

Directions:
1. Place all ingredients in a mixing bowl. Stir to combine everything.
2. Allow to marinate in the fridge for at least 30 minutes.
3. Get a foil and place the fish including the marinade in the middle of the foil.
4. Fold the foil and crimp the edges to seal.
5. Place inside the crockpot.
6. Cook on high for 2 hours or on low for 4 hours.

Nutrition Info:
- Calories per serving: 183; Carbohydrates: 2.9g; Protein: 23.4g; Fat: 11.3g; Sugar: 0.3g; Sodium: 215mg; Fiber:1.4 g

Five-spice Tilapia

Servings:4 | Cooking Time: 5 Hours

Ingredients:
- 4 tilapia fillets
- 1 teaspoon Chinese five-spice powder
- 1 tablespoon sesame oil
- ¼ cup gluten-free soy sauce
- 3 scallions, thinly sliced

Directions:
1. Season the tilapia fillets with the Chinese five-spice powder.
2. Place sesame oil in the crockpot and arrange the fish on top.
3. Cook on high for 2 hours and on low for 4 hours.
4. Halfway through the cooking time, flip the fish to slightly brown the other side.
5. Once cooking time is done, add the soy sauce and scallion and continue cooking for another hour.

Nutrition Info:
- Calories per serving: 153; Carbohydrates: 0.9g; Protein: 25.8g; Fat: 5.6g; Sugar: 0g; Sodium: 424mg; Fiber: 0g

Chili Bigeye Jack (tuna)

Servings:4 | Cooking Time: 3.5 Hours

Ingredients:
- 9 oz tuna fillet (bigeye jack), roughly chopped
- 1 teaspoon chili powder
- 1 teaspoon curry paste
- ½ cup of coconut milk
- 1 tablespoon sesame oil

Directions:
1. Mix curry paste and coconut milk and pour the liquid in the Crock Pot.
2. Add tuna fillet and sesame oil.
3. Then add chili powder.
4. Cook the meal on High for 3.5 hours.

Nutrition Info:
- Per Serving: 341 calories, 14.2g protein, 2.4g carbohydrates, 31.2g fat, 0.9g fiber, 0mg cholesterol, 11mg sodium, 91mg potassium

Cod In Lemon Sauce

Servings:4 | Cooking Time: 2.5 Hours

Ingredients:
- 4 cod fillets
- 4 tablespoons lemon juice
- 2 tablespoons olive oil
- ½ teaspoon fennel seeds
- ¼ cup of water

Directions:
1. Put the cod fillets in the Crock Pot.
2. Add water, fennel seeds, and olive oil.
3. Cook the fish on high for 2.5 hours.
4. Then transfer the fish in the bowls and sprinkle with lemon juice.

Nutrition Info:
- Per Serving: 155 calories, 20.2g protein, 0.5g carbohydrates, 8.2g fat, 0.2g fiber, 55mg cholesterol, 74mg sodium, 23mg potassium

Crockpot Smoked Trout

Servings:4 | Cooking Time: 2 Hours

Ingredients:
- 2 tablespoons liquid smoke
- 2 tablespoons olive oil
- 4 ounces smoked trout, skin removed then flaked
- Salt and pepper to taste
- 2 tablespoons mustard

Directions:
1. Place all ingredients in the crockpot.
2. Cook on high for 1 hour or on low for 2 hours until the trout flakes have absorbed the sauce.

Nutrition Info:
- Calories per serving: 116; Carbohydrates: 1.5g; Protein: 7.2g; Fat: 9.2g; Sugar: 0g; Sodium: 347mg; Fiber: 1.3g

Cilantro Haddock

Servings:2 | Cooking Time: 1.5 Hour

Ingredients:
- 6 oz haddock fillet
- 1 teaspoon dried cilantro
- 1 teaspoon olive oil
- 1 teaspoon lemon juice
- ¼ cup fish stock

Directions:
1. Heat the olive oil in the skillet well.
2. Then put the haddock fillet and roast it for 1 minute per side.
3. Transfer the fillets in the Crock Pot.
4. Add fish stock, cilantro, and lemon juice.
5. Cook the fish on high for 1.5 hours.

Nutrition Info:
- Per Serving: 121 calories, 21.3g protein, 0.1g carbohydrates, 3.4g fat, 0g fiber, 63mg cholesterol, 120mg sodium, 385mg potassium

Soy Sauce Catfish

Servings:4 | Cooking Time: 5 Hours

Ingredients:
- 1-pound catfish fillet, chopped
- ¼ cup of soy sauce
- 1 jalapeno pepper, diced
- 1 tablespoon olive oil
- 4 tablespoons fish stock

Directions:
1. Sprinkle the catfish with olive oil and put in the Crock Pot.
2. Add soy sauce, jalapeno pepper, and fish stock.
3. Close the lid and cook the meal on Low for 5 hours.

Nutrition Info:
- Per Serving: 195 calories, 19g protein, 1.4g carbohydrates, 12.3g fat, 0.2g fiber, 53mg cholesterol, 981mg sodium, 427mg potassium

Sweet Milkfish Saute

Servings:4 | Cooking Time: 3 Hours

Ingredients:
- 2 mangos, pitted, peeled, chopped
- 12 oz milkfish fillet, chopped
- ½ cup tomatoes, chopped
- ½ cup of water
- 1 teaspoon ground cardamom

Directions:
1. Mix mangos with tomatoes and ground cardamom.
2. Transfer the ingredients in the Crock Pot.
3. Then add milkfish fillet and water.
4. Cook the saute on High for 3 hours.
5. Carefully stir the saute before serving.

Nutrition Info:
- Per Serving: 268 calories, 24g protein, 26.4g carbohydrates, 8.1g fat, 3.1g fiber, 57mg cholesterol, 82mg sodium, 660mg potassium.

Miso-poached Cod

Servings:4 | Cooking Time: 2.5 Hours

Ingredients:
- 1 teaspoon miso paste
- ½ cup of water
- ½ teaspoon dried lemongrass
- 4 cod fillets
- 1 teaspoon olive oil

Directions:
1. Mix miso paste with water, dried lemongrass, and olive oil.
2. Then pour the liquid in the Crock Pot.
3. Add cod fillets.
4. Cook the cod on High for 2.5 hours.

Nutrition Info:
- Per Serving: 103 calories, 20.2g protein, 0.4g carbohydrates, 2.3g fat, 0.1g fiber, 55mg cholesterol, 124mg sodium, 5mg potassium

Salmon With Lime Butter

Servings:4 | Cooking Time: 4 Hours

Ingredients:
- 1-pound salmon fillet cut into 4 portions
- 1 tablespoon butter, melted
- Salt and pepper to taste
- 2 tablespoons lime juice
- ½ teaspoon lime zest, grated

Directions:
1. Add all ingredients in the crockpot.
2. Close the lid.
3. Cook on high for 2 hours and on low for 4 hours.

Nutrition Info:
- Calories per serving: 206; Carbohydrates: 1.8g; Protein:23.7 g; Fat: 15.2g; Sugar: 0g; Sodium:235 mg; Fiber: 0.5g

Hot Sauce Shrimps

Servings:4 | Cooking Time: 35 Minutes

Ingredients:
- 2 tablespoons hot sauce
- 1 tablespoon sunflower oil
- 4 tablespoons lemon juice
- ¼ cup of water
- 1-pound shrimps, peeled

Directions:
1. Mix shrimps with lemon juice, sunflower oil, and hot sauce. Leave them for 20 minutes to marinate.
2. After this, transfer the shrimps in the Crock Pot. Add water.
3. Cook the shrimps on High for 35 minutes.

Nutrition Info:
- Per Serving: 170 calories, 26g protein, 2.2g carbohydrates, 5.6g fat, 0.1g fiber, 239mg cholesterol, 470mg sodium, 222mg potassium

Marinara Salmon

Servings:4 | Cooking Time: 3 Hours

Ingredients:
- 1-pound salmon fillet, chopped
- ½ cup marinara sauce
- ¼ cup fresh cilantro, chopped
- ¼ cup of water

Directions:
1. Put the salmon in the Crock Pot.
2. Add marinara sauce, cilantro, and water.
3. Close the lid and cook the fish on High for 3 hours.

Nutrition Info:
- Per Serving: 177 calories, 22.6g protein, 4.3g carbohydrates, 7.9g fat, 0.8g fiber, 51mg cholesterol, 179mg sodium, 540mg potassium

Pesto Salmon

Servings:4 | Cooking Time: 2.5 Hours

Ingredients:
- 1-pound salmon fillet
- 3 tablespoons pesto sauce
- 1 tablespoon butter
- ¼ cup of water

Directions:
1. Pour water in the Crock Pot.
2. Add butter and 1 tablespoon of pesto.
3. Add salmon and cook the fish on High for 2.5 hours.
4. Chop the cooked salmon and top with remaining pesto sauce.

Nutrition Info:
- Per Serving: 226 calories, 23.2g protein, 0.8g carbohydrates, 14.8g fat, 0.2g fiber, 60mg cholesterol, 142mg sodium, 436mg potassium

Crab Legs

Servings: 4 | Cooking Time: 1 Hour And 30 Minutes

Ingredients:
- 4 pounds king crab legs, broken in half
- 3 lemon wedges
- ¼ cup butter, melted
- ½ cup chicken stock

Directions:

1. In your Crock Pot, mix stock with crab legs and butter, cover and cook on High for 1 hour and 30 minutes.
2. Divide crab legs between bowls, drizzle melted butter all over and serve with lemon wedges on the side.

Nutrition Info:
- calories 100, fat 1, fiber 5, carbs 12, protein 3

Ginger Cod

Servings:6 | Cooking Time: 5 Hours

Ingredients:
- 6 cod fillets
- 1 teaspoon minced ginger
- 1 tablespoon olive oil
- ¼ teaspoon minced garlic
- ¼ cup chicken stock

Directions:

1. In the mixing bowl mix minced ginger with olive oil and minced garlic.
2. Gently rub the fish fillets with the ginger mixture and put in the Crock Pot.
3. Add chicken stock.
4. Cook the cod on Low for 5 hours.

Nutrition Info:
- Per Serving: 112 calories, 20.1g protein, 0.3g carbohydrates, 3.4g fat, 0g fiber, 55mg cholesterol, 102mg sodium, 5mg potassium

Chapter 7 Lunch & Dinner Recipes

Chapter 7 Lunch & Dinner Recipes

Pesto Freekeh

Servings:4 | Cooking Time: 2 Hours

Ingredients:
- 2 tablespoons pesto sauce
- 1 tablespoon sesame oil
- 1 oz raisins
- 1 cup freekeh
- 3 cups chicken stock

Directions:
1. Pour the chicken stock in the Crock Pot.
2. Add freekeh and raisins and cook the ingredients on High for 2 hours. The cooked freekeh should be tender.
3. Then transfer the freekeh mixture in the bowl.
4. Add sesame oil and pesto sauce.
5. Carefully mix the meal.

Nutrition Info:
- Per Serving: 125 calories, 3.5g protein, 13.2g carbohydrates, 7.4g fat, 1.4g fiber, 2mg cholesterol, 621mg sodium, 64mg potassium.

Buttered Broccoli

Servings: 4 | Cooking Time: 1 1/2 Hours

Ingredients:
- 2 heads broccoli, cut into florets
- 1 shallot, sliced
- 2 garlic cloves, chopped
- 4 tablespoons butter
- Salt and pepper to taste

Directions:
1. Combine all the ingredients in your Crock Pot.
2. Add enough salt and pepper and cook the broccoli on high settings for 1 1/4 hours.
3. Serve the broccoli warm and fresh.

Sweet Farro

Servings:3 | Cooking Time: 6 Hours

Ingredients:
- ½ cup farro
- 2 cups of water
- ½ cup heavy cream
- 2 tablespoons dried cranberries
- 2 tablespoons sugar

Directions:
1. Chop the cranberries and put in the Crock Pot.
2. Add water, heavy cream, sugar, and farro.
3. Mix the ingredients with the help of the spoon and close the lid.
4. Cook the farro on low for 6 hours.

Nutrition Info:
- Per Serving: 208 calories, 5.1g protein, 31g carbohydrates, 7.4g fat, 2.2g fiber, 27mg cholesterol, 32mg sodium, 24mg potassium.

Cauliflower Mashed Sweet Potato

Servings: 6 | Cooking Time: 6 1/4 Hours

Ingredients:
- 1 head cauliflower, cut into florets
- 1 pound sweet potatoes, peeled and cubed
- 1 shallot, chopped
- 2 garlic cloves, chopped
- 1 cup vegetable stock
- Salt and pepper to taste

Directions:
1. Combine all the ingredients in your Crock Pot.
2. Add salt and pepper to taste and cook on low settings for 6 hours.
3. When done, mash the mix with a potato masher and serve warm.

Cod And Asparagus

Servings: 4 | Cooking Time: 2 Hours

Ingredients:
- 4 cod fillets, boneless
- 1 bunch asparagus
- 12 tablespoons lemon juice
- Salt and black pepper to the taste
- 2 tablespoons olive oil

Directions:
1. Divide cod fillets between tin foil pieces, top each with asparagus spears, lemon juice, lemon pepper and oil and wrap them.
2. Arrange wrapped fish in your Crock Pot, cover and cook on High for 2 hours.
3. Unwrap fish, divide it and asparagus between plates and serve for lunch.

Nutrition Info:
- calories 202, fat 3, fiber 6, carbs 7, protein 3

Three Pepper Roasted Pork Tenderloin

Servings: 8 | Cooking Time: 8 1/4 Hours

Ingredients:
- 3 pounds pork tenderloin
- 2 tablespoons Dijon mustard
- 1/4 cup three pepper mix
- Salt and pepper to taste
- 1 cup chicken stock

Directions:
1. Season the pork with salt and pepper.
2. Brush the meat with mustard. Spread the pepper mix on your chopping board then roll the pork through this mixture, making sure to coat it well.
3. Place carefully in your crock pot and pour in the stock.
4. Cook on low settings for 8 hours.
5. Serve the pork tenderloin sliced and warm with your favorite side dish.

Mango Chutney Pork Chops

Servings: 4 | Cooking Time: 5 1/4 Hours

Ingredients:
- 4 pork chops
- 1 jar mango chutney
- 3/4 cup chicken stock
- 1 bay leaf
- Salt and pepper to taste

Directions:
1. Combine all the ingredients in your crock pot.
2. Add enough salt and pepper and cook on low settings for 5 hours.
3. Serve the pork chops warm.

Salted Caramel Rice Pudding

Servings:2 | Cooking Time: 3 Hours

Ingredients:
- 2 teaspoons salted caramel
- ½ cup basmati rice
- 1.5 cup milk
- 1 teaspoon vanilla extract

Directions:
1. Pour milk in the Crock Pot.
2. Add vanilla extract and basmati rice.
3. Cook the rice on high or 3 hours.
4. Then add salted caramel and carefully mix the pudding.
5. Cool it to the room temperature and transfer in the bowls.

Nutrition Info:
- Per Serving: 284 calories, 9.8g protein, 48.9g carbohydrates, 4.7g fat, 0.8g fiber, 16mg cholesterol, 99mg sodium, 161mg potassium.

Crock Pot Steamed Rice

Servings: 8 | Cooking Time: 4 Hours

Ingredients:
- 2 cups white rice
- 4 cups water
- 1 bay leaf
- Salt and pepper to taste

Directions:
1. Combine all the ingredients in your crock pot.
2. Add salt and pepper as needed and cook on low

settings for 4 hours. If possible, stir once during the cooking process.

3. Serve the rice warm or chilled, as a side dish to your favorite veggie main dish.

Beans And Peas Bowl

Servings:4 | Cooking Time: 6 Hours

Ingredients:
- ½ cup black beans, soaked
- 1 cup green peas
- 4 cups of water
- 1 tablespoon tomato paste
- 1 teaspoon sriracha

Directions:
1. Pour water in the Crock Pot.
2. Add black beans and cook them for 5 hours on High.
3. Then add green peas, tomato paste, and sriracha.
4. Stir the ingredients and cook the meal for 1 hour on High.

Nutrition Info:
- Per Serving: 117 calories, 7.4g protein, 21.4g carbohydrates, 0.5g fat, 5.7g fiber, 0mg cholesterol, 23mg sodium, 491mg potassium.

Green Lentils Salad

Servings:2 | Cooking Time: 4 Hours

Ingredients:
- ¼ cup green lentils
- 1 cup chicken stock
- ½ teaspoon ground cumin
- 2 cups lettuce, chopped
- ¼ cup Greek Yogurt

Directions:
1. Mix green lentils with chicken stock and transfer in the Crock Pot.
2. Cook the ingredients on High for 4 hours.
3. Then cool the lentils and transfer them in the salad bowl.
4. Add ground cumin, lettuce, and Greek yogurt.
5. Mix the salad carefully.

Nutrition Info:
- Per Serving: 118 calories, 9.4g protein, 17.7g carbohydrates, 1.3g fat, 7.7g fiber, 1mg cholesterol, 395mg sodium, 359mg potassium.

Fragrant Turmeric Beans

Servings:4 | Cooking Time: 8 Hours

Ingredients:
- 1 jalapeno pepper, sliced
- 1 oz fresh ginger, grated
- 1 teaspoon ground turmeric
- 2 cups black beans, soaked
- 5 cups chicken stock

Directions:
1. Put black beans in the Crock Pot.
2. Add jalapeno pepper, ginger, ground turmeric, and chicken stock.
3. Cook the meal on low for 8 hours.

Nutrition Info:
- Per Serving: 371 calories, 22.5g protein, 67g carbohydrates, 2.6g fat, 15.9g fiber, 0mg cholesterol, 962mg sodium, 1573mg potassium.

Asparagus Casserole

Servings: 6 | Cooking Time: 6 1/2 Hours

Ingredients:
- 1 bunch asparagus, trimmed and chopped
- 1 can condensed cream of mushroom soup
- 2 hard-boiled eggs, peeled and cubed
- 1 cup grated Cheddar
- 2 cups bread croutons
- Salt and pepper to taste

Directions:
1. Combine the asparagus, mushroom soup, hard-boiled eggs, cheese and bread croutons in your Crock Pot.
2. Add salt and pepper to taste and cook on low settings for 6 hours.
3. Serve the casserole warm and fresh.

Tomato Soy Glazed Chicken

Servings: 8 | Cooking Time: 8 1/4 Hours

Ingredients:
- 8 chicken thighs
- 1/2 cup soy sauce
- 2 tablespoons brown sugar
- 1 teaspoon chili powder
- 1/2 cup tomato sauce

Directions:

1. Combine all the ingredients in your crock pot.
2. Cook the chicken on low settings for 8 hours.
3. Serve the chicken warm and fresh.

Cheesy Chicken

Servings: 2 | Cooking Time: 2 1/4 Hours

Ingredients:
- 2 chicken breasts
- 1 cup cream of chicken soup
- 1 cup grated Cheddar
- 1/4 teaspoon garlic powder
- Salt and pepper to taste

Directions:
1. Combine all the ingredients in your crock pot.
2. Add salt and pepper to taste and cover with a lid.
3. Cook on high settings for 2 hours.
4. Serve the chicken warm, topped with plenty of cheesy sauce.

Apple Cups

Servings:2 | Cooking Time: 6 Hours

Ingredients:
- 2 green apples
- 3 oz white rice
- 1 shallot, diced
- ¼ cup of water
- 1 tablespoon cream cheese

Directions:
1. Scoop the flesh from the apples to make the apple cups.
2. Then mix the onion with rice, and curry paste.
3. Pour water in the Crock Pot.
4. Fill the apple cups with rice mixture and top with cream cheese,
5. Then combine the raisins, diced onion, white rice, salt, and curry.
6. Cook the meal on Low for 6 hours.

Nutrition Info:
- Per Serving: 292 calories, 4.1g protein, 65.8g carbohydrates, 2.4g fat, 6g fiber, 6mg cholesterol, 20mg sodium, 310mg potassium.

Oregano Millet

Servings:3 | Cooking Time: 3 Hours

Ingredients:
- ¼ cup heavy cream
- ½ cup millet
- 1 teaspoon dried oregano
- 1 cup of water

Directions:
1. Put all ingredients from the list above in the Crock Pot.
2. Close the lid and cook on high for 3 hours.

Nutrition Info:
- Per Serving: 162 calories, 3.9g protein, 24.9g carbohydrates, 5.2g fat, 3g fiber, 14mg cholesterol, 6mg sodium, 81mg potassium.

Milky Semolina

Servings:2 | Cooking Time: 1 Hour

Ingredients:
- ¼ cup semolina
- 1 ½ cup milk
- 1 teaspoon vanilla extract
- 1 teaspoon sugar

Directions:
1. Put all ingredients in the Crock Pot.
2. Close the lid and cook the semolina on high for 1 hour.
3. When the meal is cooked, carefully stir it and cool it to room temperature.

Nutrition Info:
- Per Serving: 180 calories, 8.7g protein, 26.5g carbohydrates, 4g fat, 0.8g fiber, 15mg cholesterol, 87mg sodium, 147mg potassium.

Creamed Sweet Corn

Servings: 6 | Cooking Time: 3 1/4 Hours

Ingredients:
- 2 cans (15 oz.) sweet corn, drained
- 1 cup cream cheese
- 1 cup grated Cheddar cheese
- 1/2 cup heavy cream
- Salt and pepper to taste
- 1 pinch nutmeg

Directions:

1. Combine the corn, cream cheese, Cheddar and cream in your Crock Pot.
2. Add the nutmeg, salt and pepper and cook on low settings for 3 hours.
3. Serve the creamed corn warm.

Parmesan Artichokes

Servings: 2 | Cooking Time: 4 1/4 Hours

Ingredients:
- 2 large artichokes
- 1/4 cup breadcrumbs
- 1/2 cup grated Parmesan
- 1/2 cup vegetable stock

Directions:
1. Cut and clean the artichokes.
2. Mix the breadcrumbs and cheese in a bowl.
3. Top each artichoke with this mixture and rub it well to make sure it sticks to the artichoke.
4. Place the artichokes in a crock pot and add the stock.
5. Cook on low settings for 4 hours.
6. Serve the artichokes warm.

Ginger Glazed Tofu

Servings: 6 | Cooking Time: 2 1/4 Hours

Ingredients:
- 12 oz. firm tofu, cubed
- 1 tablespoon hot sauce
- 1 teaspoon grated ginger
- 2 tablespoons soy sauce
- 1/2 cup vegetable stock

Directions:
1. Season the tofu with hot sauce, ginger and soy sauce. Place the tofu in your crock pot.
2. Add the stock and cook on high settings for 2 hours.
3. Serve the tofu warm with your favorite side dish.

Cumin Rice

Servings:6 | Cooking Time: 3.5 Hours

Ingredients:
- 2 cups long-grain rice
- 5 cups chicken stock
- 1 teaspoon cumin seeds
- 1 teaspoon olive oil

- 1 tablespoon cream cheese

Directions:
1. Heat the olive oil in the skillet.
2. Add cumin seeds and roast them for 2-3 minutes.
3. Then transfer the roasted cumin seeds in the Crock Pot.
4. Add rice and chickens tock. Gently stir the ingredients.
5. Close the lid and cook the rice on high for 3.5 hours.
6. Then add cream cheese and stir the rice well.

Nutrition Info:
- Per Serving: 247 calories, 5.2g protein, 50.1g carbohydrates, 2.3g fat, 0.8g fiber, 2mg cholesterol, 645mg sodium, 91mg potassium.

Sweet Popcorn

Servings:4 | Cooking Time: 20 Minutes

Ingredients:
- 2 cups popped popcorn
- 2 tablespoons butter
- 2 tablespoons brown sugar
- ½ teaspoon ground cinnamon

Directions:
1. Put butter and sugar in the Crock Pot.
2. Add ground cinnamon and cook the mixture on High or 15 minutes.
3. Then open the lid, stir the mixture, and add popped popcorn.
4. Carefully mix the ingredients with the help of the spatula and cook on high for 5 minutes more.

Nutrition Info:
- Per Serving: 84 calories, 0.6g protein, 7.8g carbohydrates, 5.9g fat, 0.7g fiber, 15mg cholesterol, 43mg sodium, 22mg potassium.

Butter Pink Rice

Servings:6 | Cooking Time: 5.5 Hours

Ingredients:
- 1 cup pink rice
- 1 cups chicken stock
- 1 teaspoon cream cheese
- 1 tablespoon butter

Directions:
1. Put all ingredients in the Crock Pot and stir gently.

2. Close the lid and cook the meal on low for 5.5 hours.

Nutrition Info:
• Per Serving: 122 calories, 2.2g protein, 22.3g carbohydrates, 3g fat, 1g fiber, 6mg cholesterol, 143mg sodium, 52mg potassium.

Eggplant Parmigiana

Servings: 6 | Cooking Time: 8 1/4 Hours

Ingredients:
• 4 medium eggplants, peeled and finely sliced
• 1/4 cup all-purpose flour
• 4 cups marinara sauce
• 1 cup grated Parmesan
• Salt and pepper to taste

Directions:
1. Season the eggplants with salt and pepper and sprinkle with flour.
2. Layer the eggplant slices and marinara sauce in your crock pot.
3. Top with the grated cheese and cook on low settings for 8 hours.
4. Serve the parmigiana warm or chilled.

Coffee Beef Roast

Servings: 6 | Cooking Time: 4 1/4 Hours

Ingredients:
• 2 pounds beef sirloin
• 2 tablespoons olive oil
• 4 garlic cloves, minced
• 1 cup strong brewed coffee
• 1/2 cup beef stock
• Salt and pepper to taste

Directions:
1. Combine all the ingredients in your crock pot, adding salt and pepper to taste.
2. Cover with a lid and cook on high settings for 4 hours.
3. Serve the roast warm and fresh with your favorite side dish.

Ginger Slow Roasted Pork

Servings: 8 | Cooking Time: 7 1/4 Hours

Ingredients:
• 4 pounds pork shoulder
• 2 teaspoons grated ginger
• 1 tablespoon soy sauce
• 1 tablespoon honey
• 1 1/2 cups vegetables stock
• Salt and pepper to taste

Directions:
1. Season the pork with salt and pepper, as well as ginger, soy sauce and honey.
2. Place the pork in your Crock Pot and add the stock.
3. Cover and cook on low settings for 7 hours.
4. Serve the pork warm with your favorite side dish.

Bacon Millet

Servings:6 | Cooking Time: 6 Hours

Ingredients:
• 2 cups millet
• 4 cups of water
• 2 tablespoons butter
• ½ teaspoon salt
• 2 oz bacon, chopped, cooked

Directions:
1. Put millet and salt in the Crock Pot.
2. Add water and cook the meal on low for 6 hours.
3. When the millet is cooked, carefully mix it with butter and transfer in the plates.
4. Add bacon.

Nutrition Info:
• Per Serving: 337 calories, 10.9g protein, 48.7g carbohydrates, 10.6g fat, 5.7g fiber, 21mg cholesterol, 447mg sodium, 186mg potassium.

French Onion Sandwich Filling

Servings: 10 | Cooking Time: 9 1/4 Hours

Ingredients:
• 4 pounds beef roast
• 4 sweet onions, sliced
• 4 bacon slices, chopped
• 1 teaspoon garlic powder
• 1/2 cup white wine
• Salt and pepper to taste

- 1 thyme sprig

Directions:
1. Combine all the ingredients in your crock pot.
2. Add salt and pepper to taste and cook on low settings for 9 hours.
3. When done, shred the meat into fine threads and use it as sandwich filling, warm or chilled.

Cherry Rice

Servings:4 | Cooking Time: 3 Hours

Ingredients:
- 1 cup basmati rice
- 1 cup cherries, raw
- 3 cups of water
- 2 tablespoons of liquid honey
- 1 tablespoon butter, melted

Directions:
1. Put cherries and rice in the Crock Pot.
2. Add water and cook the meal on high for 3 hours.
3. Meanwhile, mix liquid honey and butter.
4. When the rice is cooked, add liquid honey mixture and carefully stir.

Nutrition Info:
- Per Serving: 249 calories, 3.9g protein, 51.1g carbohydrates, 3.3g fat, 1.4g fiber, 8mg cholesterol, 29mg sodium, 136mg potassium.

Cauliflower Mashed Potatoes

Servings: 4 | Cooking Time: 4 1/2 Hours

Ingredients:
- 1 pound potatoes, peeled and cubed
- 2 cups cauliflower florets
- 1/4 cup vegetable stock
- 2 tablespoons coconut oil
- 1/4 cup coconut milk
- Salt and pepper to taste

Directions:
1. Combine the potatoes, cauliflower, stock, coconut oil and coconut milk in your Crock Pot.
2. Add salt and pepper to taste and cook on low settings for 4 hours.
3. When done, mash with a potato masher and serve right away.

Apricot Glazed Gammon

Servings: 6-8

Cooking Time: 6 1/4 Hours

Ingredients:
- 3-4 pounds piece of gammon joint
- 1/2 cup apricot preserve
- 1 teaspoon cumin powder
- 1/4 teaspoon chili powder
- 1 cup vegetable stock
- Salt and pepper to taste

Directions:
1. Mix the apricot preserve with cumin powder and chili powder then spread this mixture over the gammon.
2. Place the meat in your Crock Pot and add the stock.
3. Cook on low settings for 6 hours.
4. Serve the gammon with your favorite side dish, warm or chilled.

Red Salsa Chicken

Servings: 8 | Cooking Time: 8 1/4 Hours

Ingredients:
- 8 chicken thighs
- 2 cups red salsa
- 1/2 cup chicken stock
- 1 cup grated Cheddar cheese
- Salt and pepper to taste

Directions:
1. Combine the chicken with the salsa and stock in your Crock Pot.
2. Add the cheese and cook on low settings for 8 hours.
3. Serve the chicken warm with your favorite side dish.

Cider Braised Chicken

Servings: 8 | Cooking Time: 8 1/4 Hours

Ingredients:
- 1 whole chicken, cut into smaller pieces
- Salt and pepper to taste
- 1 teaspoon dried thyme
- 1 teaspoon dried oregano
- 1 teaspoon cumin powder
- Salt to taste
- 1 1/2 cups apple cider

Directions:
1. Season the chicken with salt, thyme, oregano and cumin powder and place it in your crock pot.
2. Add the apple cider and cook on low settings for 8 hours.
3. Serve the chicken warm with your favorite side dish.

Butter Buckwheat

Servings:4 | Cooking Time: 4 Hours

Ingredients:
- 2 tablespoons butter
- 1 cup buckwheat
- 2 cups chicken stock
- ½ teaspoon salt

Directions:
1. Mix buckwheat with salt and transfer in the Crock Pot.
2. Add chicken stock and close the lid.
3. Cook the buckwheat on High for 4 hours.
4. Then add butter, carefully mixture the buckwheat, and transfer in the bowls.

Nutrition Info:
- Per Serving: 202 calories, 6g protein, 30.8g carbohydrates, 7.5g fat, 4.3g fiber, 15mg cholesterol, 714mg sodium, 205mg potassium.

Bacon Brussels Sprouts

Servings: 6 | Cooking Time: 6 1/4 Hours

Ingredients:
- 2 pounds Brussels sprouts, halved
- 6 bacon slices, chopped
- 1/2 cup vegetable stock
- Salt and pepper to taste

Directions:
1. Cook the bacon in a skillet until crisp.
2. Combine all the ingredients in your crock pot, adding salt and pepper to taste.
3. Cook on low settings for 6 hours.
4. Serve the sprouts warm or chilled.

Chicken Drumsticks And Buffalo Sauce

Servings: 2 | Cooking Time: 8 Hours

Ingredients:
- 1 pound chicken drumsticks
- 2 tablespoons buffalo wing sauce
- ½ cup chicken stock
- 2 tablespoons honey
- 1 teaspoon lemon juice
- Salt and black pepper to the taste

Directions:
1. In your Crock Pot, mix the chicken with the sauce and the other ingredients, toss, put the lid on and cook on Low for 8 hours.
2. Divide everything between plates and serve.

Nutrition Info:
- calories 361, fat 7, fiber 8, carbs 18, protein 22

French Onion Roasted Pork Chop

Servings: 6 | Cooking Time: 6 1/4 Hours

Ingredients:
- 6 pork chops
- 1/4 cup white wine
- 1 can condensed onion soup
- 1 teaspoon garlic powder
- Salt and pepper to taste

Directions:
1. Combine all the ingredients in your Crock Pot.
2. Add salt and pepper to taste and cover with a lid.
3. Cook on low settings for 6 hours.
4. Serve the pork chops warm.

Blue Cheese Chicken

Servings: 4 | Cooking Time: 2 1/4 Hours

Ingredients:
- 4 chicken breasts
- 1 teaspoon dried oregano
- Salt and pepper to taste
- 1/2 cup crumbled blue cheese
- 1/2 cup chicken stock

Directions:
1. Season the chicken with salt and pepper and place it in your crock pot.
2. Add the stock then top each piece of chicken with

crumbled feta cheese.
3. Cook on high settings for 2 hours.
4. Serve the chicken warm.

Chicken Pilaf

Servings:3 | Cooking Time: 6 Hours

Ingredients:
- ½ cup basmati rice
- 2 cups of water
- 5 oz chicken fillet, chopped
- 1 teaspoon chili powder
- ½ teaspoon salt

Directions:
1. Put the rice and chicken fillet in the Crock Pot.
2. Add chili powder, salt, and water. Carefully stir the ingredients and close the lid.
3. Cook the pilaf on Low for 6 hours.

Nutrition Info:
- Per Serving: 205 calories, 16g protein, 25.1g carbohydrates, 3.9g fat, 0.7g fiber, 42mg cholesterol, 443mg sodium, 169mg potassium.

Creamy Polenta

Servings:4 | Cooking Time: 2.5 Hours

Ingredients:
- 1 cup polenta
- 3 cups of water
- 1 cup heavy cream
- 1 teaspoon salt

Directions:
1. Put all ingredients in the Crock Pot.
2. Close the lid and cook them on High for 5 hours.
3. When the polenta is cooked, stir it carefully and transfer it in the serving plates.

Nutrition Info:
- Per Serving: 242 calories, 3.5g protein, 31.3g carbohydrates, 11.4g fat, 1g fiber, 41mg cholesterol, 600mg sodium, 24mg potassium.

Beans-rice Mix

Servings:4 | Cooking Time: 3 Hours

Ingredients:
- 5 oz red kidney beans, canned
- 1 teaspoon garlic powder
- ¼ teaspoon ground coriander
- ½ cup long-grain rice
- 2 cups chicken stock

Directions:
1. Put long-grain rice in the Crock Pot.
2. Add chicken stock, ground coriander, and garlic powder.
3. Close the lid and cook the rice for 2.5 hours on High.
4. Then add red kidney beans, stir the mixture, and cook for 30 minutes in High.

Nutrition Info:
- Per Serving: 211 calories, 10.1g protein, 41.1g carbohydrates, 0.8g fat, 5.8g fiber, 0mg cholesterol, 387mg sodium, 523mg potassium.

Green Enchilada Pork Roast

Servings: 8 | Cooking Time: 8 1/4 Hours

Ingredients:
- 4 pounds pork roast
- 2 cups green enchilada sauce
- 1/2 cup chopped cilantro
- 2 chipotle peppers, chopped
- 1/2 cup vegetable stock
- Salt and pepper to taste

Directions:
1. Combine the enchilada sauce, cilantro, chipotle peppers and stock in your Crock Pot.
2. Add the pork roast and season with salt and pepper.
3. Cook on low settings for 8 hours.
4. Serve the pork warm with your favorite side dish.

Mushroom Rissoto

Servings:4 | Cooking Time: 2.5 Hours

Ingredients:
- 1 cup cremini mushrooms, chopped
- 1 tablespoon cream cheese
- 1 cup basmati rice
- 1.5 cups chicken stock

Directions:
1. Put basmati rice and chicken stock in the Crock Pot.
2. Add cremini mushrooms and close the lid.
3. Cook the risotto on High for 2 hours.
4. Then add cream cheese and stir the rice. Cook it on high for 30 minutes more.

Nutrition Info:
- Per Serving: 186 calories, 4.2g protein, 38.1g carbohydrates, 1.4g fat, 0.7g fiber, 3mg cholesterol, 297mg sodium, 142mg potassium

Mustard Short Ribs

Servings: 2 | Cooking Time: 8 Hours

Ingredients:
- 2 beef short ribs, bone in and cut into individual ribs
- Salt and black pepper to the taste
- ½ cup BBQ sauce
- 1 tablespoon mustard
- 1 tablespoon green onions, chopped

Directions:
1. In your Crock Pot, mix the ribs with the sauce and the other ingredients, toss, put the lid on and cook on Low for 8 hours.
2. Divide the mix between plates and serve.

Nutrition Info:
- calories 284, fat 7, 4, carbs 18, protein 20

Deviled Chicken

Servings: 4 | Cooking Time: 6 1/4 Hours

Ingredients:
- 4 chicken breasts
- 1 cup tomato sauce
- 1/2 cup hot sauce
- 2 tablespoons butter
- 4 garlic cloves, minced
- Salt and pepper to taste

Directions:
1. Combine all the ingredients in your crock pot.
2. Add salt and pepper and cover with a lid.
3. Cook on low settings for 6 hours.
4. Serve the chicken warm and fresh.

Chapter 8 Vegetable & Vegetarian Recipes

Chapter 8 Vegetable & Vegetarian Recipes

Garlic Gnocchi

Servings:4 | Cooking Time: 3 Hours

Ingredients:
- 2 cups mozzarella, shredded
- 3 egg yolks, beaten
- 1 teaspoon garlic, minced
- ½ cup heavy cream
- Salt and pepper to taste

Directions:
1. In a mixing bowl, combine the mozzarella and egg yolks.
2. Form gnocchi balls and place in the fridge to set.
3. Boil a pot of water over high flame and drop the gnocchi balls for 30 seconds. Take them out and transfer to the crockpot.
4. Into the crockpot add the garlic and heavy cream.
5. Season with salt and pepper to taste.
6. Close the lid and cook on low for 3 hours or on high for 1 hour.

Nutrition Info:
- Calories per serving: 178; Carbohydrates: 4.1g; Protein:20.5 g; Fat: 8.9g; Sugar:0.3g; Sodium: 421mg; Fiber: 2.1g

Garlic Butter

Servings:8 | Cooking Time: 20 Minutes

Ingredients:
- 1 cup vegan butter
- 1 tablespoon garlic powder
- ¼ cup fresh dill, chopped

Directions:
1. Put all ingredients in the Crock Pot and cook on High for 20 minutes.
2. Then pour the liquid in the ice cubes molds and refrigerate for 30 minutes or until butter is solid.

Nutrition Info:
- Per Serving: 211 calories, 0.7g protein, 1.6g carbohydrates, 23.1g fat, 0.3g fiber, 61mg cholesterol, 167mg sodium, 68mg potassium.

Cauliflower Rice

Servings:6 | Cooking Time: 2 Hours

Ingredients:
- 4 cups cauliflower, shredded
- 1 cup vegetable stock
- 1 cup of water
- 1 tablespoon cream cheese
- 1 teaspoon dried oregano

Directions:
1. Put all ingredients in the Crock Pot.
2. Close the lid and cook the cauliflower rice on High for 2 hours.

Nutrition Info:
- Per Serving: 25 calories, 0.8g protein, 3.9g carbohydrates, 0.8g fat, 1.8g fiber, 2mg cholesterol, 153mg sodium, 211mg potassium

Mushroom Steaks

Servings:4 | Cooking Time: 2 Hours

Ingredients:
- 4 Portobello mushrooms
- 1 tablespoon avocado oil
- 1 tablespoon lemon juice
- 2 tablespoons coconut cream
- ½ teaspoon ground black pepper

Directions:
1. Slice Portobello mushrooms into steaks and sprinkle with avocado oil, lemon juice, coconut cream, and ground black pepper.
2. Then arrange the mushroom steaks in the Crock Pot in one layer (you will need to cook all mushroom steaks by 2 times).
3. Cook the meal on High for 1 hour.

Nutrition Info:
- Per Serving: 43 calories, 3.3g protein, 3.9g carbohydrates, 2.3g fat, 1.4g fiber, 0mg cholesterol, 2mg sodium, 339mg potassium.

Carrot Strips

Servings:2 | Cooking Time: 1 Hour

Ingredients:
- 2 carrots, peeled
- 2 tablespoons sunflower oil
- 1 teaspoon dried thyme
- ½ teaspoon salt
- ½ cup of water

Directions:
1. Cut the carrots into the strips.
2. Then heat the sunflower oil in the skillet until hot.
3. Put the carrot strips in the hot oil and roast for 2-3 minutes per side.
4. Pour water in the Crock Pot.
5. Add salt and dried thyme.
6. Then add roasted carrot and cook the meal on High for 1 hour.

Nutrition Info:
- Per Serving: 150 calories, 0.6g protein, 6.3g carbohydrates, 14g fat, 1.7g fiber, 0mg cholesterol, 625mg sodium, 200mg potassium.

Ranch Broccoli

Servings:3 | Cooking Time: 1.5 Hours

Ingredients:
- 3 cups broccoli
- 1 teaspoon chili flakes
- 2 tablespoons ranch dressing
- 2 cups of water

Directions:
1. Put the broccoli in the Crock Pot.
2. Add water and close the lid.
3. Cook the broccoli on high for 1.5 hours.
4. Then drain water and transfer the broccoli in the bowl.
5. Sprinkle it with chili flakes and ranch dressing. Shake the meal gently.

Nutrition Info:
- Per Serving: 34 calories, 2.7g protein, 6.6g carbohydrates, 0.3g fat, 2.4g fiber, 0mg cholesterol, 91mg sodium, 291mg potassium.

Crockpot Baked Tofu

Servings:4 | Cooking Time: 2 Hours

Ingredients:
- 1 small package extra firm tofu, sliced
- 3 tablespoons soy sauce
- 1 tablespoon sesame oil
- 2 teaspoons minced garlic
- Juice from ½ lemon, freshly squeezed

Directions:
1. In a deep dish, mix together the soy sauce, sesame oil, garlic, and lemon. Add a few tablespoons of water if the sauce is too thick.
2. Marinate the tofu slices for at least 2 hours.
3. Line the crockpot with foil and grease it with cooking spray.
4. Place the slices of marinated tofu into the crockpot.
5. Cook on low for 4 hours or on high for 2 hours.
6. Make sure that the tofu slices have a crispy outer texture.

Nutrition Info:
- Calories per serving:145; Carbohydrates: 4.1g; Protein: 11.6g; Fat: 10.8g; Sugar: 0.6g; Sodium: 142mg; Fiber:1.5 g

Sautéed Endives

Servings:4 | Cooking Time: 40 Minutes

Ingredients:
- 1-pound endives, roughly chopped
- ½ cup of water
- 1 tablespoon avocado oil
- 1 teaspoon garlic, diced
- 2 tablespoons coconut cream

Directions:
1. Pour water in the Crock Pot.
2. Add endives and garlic.
3. Close the lid and cook them on High for 30 minutes.
4. Then add coconut cream and avocado oil.
5. Cook the endives for 10 minutes more.

Nutrition Info:
- Per Serving: 42 calories, 1.9g protein, 4.4g carbohydrates, 2.4g fat, 3.7g fiber, 6mg cholesterol, 41mg sodium, 376mg potassium.

Green Peas Puree

Servings:2 | Cooking Time: 1 Hour

Ingredients:
- 2 cups green peas, frozen
- 1 tablespoon coconut oil
- 1 teaspoon smoked paprika
- 1 cup vegetable stock

Directions:
1. Put green peas, smoked paprika, and vegetable stock in the Crock Pot.
2. Cook the ingredients in high for 1 hour.
3. Then drain the liquid and mash the green peas with the help of the potato masher.
4. Add coconut oil and carefully stir the cooked puree.

Nutrition Info:
- Per Serving: 184 calories, 8.4g protein, 21.9g carbohydrates, 7.8g fat, 7.8g fiber, 0mg cholesterol, 389mg sodium, 386mg potassium.

Creamy Puree

Servings:4 | Cooking Time: 4 Hours

Ingredients:
- 2 cups potatoes, chopped
- 3 cups of water
- 1 tablespoon vegan butter
- ¼ cup cream
- 1 teaspoon salt

Directions:
1. Pour water in the Crock Pot.
2. Add potatoes and salt.
3. Cook the vegetables on high for 4 hours.
4. Then drain water, add butter, and cream.
5. Mash the potatoes until smooth.

Nutrition Info:
- Per Serving: 87 calories, 1.4g protein, 12.3g carbohydrates, 3.8g fat, 1.8g fiber, 10mg cholesterol, 617mg sodium, 314mg potassium

Tomato Okra

Servings:2 | Cooking Time: 6 Hours

Ingredients:
- 2 cups okra, sliced
- 1 teaspoon chili powder
- 1 teaspoon salt
- 1 cup tomato juice
- ¼ cup fresh parsley, chopped

Directions:
1. Put all ingredients in the Crock Pot and carefully mix.
2. Close the lid and cook the okra on Low for 6 hours.

Nutrition Info:
- Per Serving: 67 calories, 3.2g protein, 13.8g carbohydrates, 0.5g fat, 4.4g fiber, 0mg cholesterol, 1514mg sodium, 644mg potassium.

Garlic Sweet Potato

Servings:4 | Cooking Time: 6 Hours

Ingredients:
- 2-pounds sweet potatoes, chopped
- 1 teaspoon minced garlic
- 2 tablespoons vegan butter
- 1 teaspoon salt
- 3 cups of water

Directions:
1. Pour water in the Crock Pot. Add sweet potatoes.
2. Then add salt and close the lid.
3. Cook the sweet potato on Low for 6 hours.
4. After this, drain the water and transfer the vegetables in the big bowl.
5. Add minced garlic and butter. Carefully stir the sweet potatoes until butter is melted.

Nutrition Info:
- Per Serving: 320 calories, 3.6g protein, 63.5g carbohydrates, 6.2g fat, 9.3g fiber, 15mg cholesterol, 648mg sodium, 1857mg potassium.

Mashed Turnips

Servings:6 | Cooking Time: 7 Hours

Ingredients:
- 3-pounds turnip, chopped
- 3 cups of water
- 1 tablespoon vegan butter
- 1 tablespoon chives, chopped
- 2 oz Parmesan, grated

Directions:
1. Put turnips in the Crock Pot.
2. Add water and cook the vegetables on low for 7 hours.
3. Then drain water and mash the turnips.
4. Add chives, butter, and Parmesan.
5. Carefully stir the mixture until butter and Parmesan are melted.
6. Then add chives. Mix the mashed turnips again.

Nutrition Info:
- Per Serving: 162 calories, 8.6g protein, 15.1g carbohydrates, 8.1g fat, 4.1g fiber, 22mg cholesterol, 475mg sodium, 490mg potassium.

Chili Dip

Servings:5 | Cooking Time: 5 Hours

Ingredients:
- 5 oz chilies, canned, chopped
- 3 oz Mozzarella, shredded
- 1 tomato, chopped
- ½ cup milk
- 1 teaspoon cornflour

Directions:
1. Mix milk with cornflour and whisk until smooth. Pour the liquid in the Crock Pot.
2. Then add chilies, Mozzarella, and tomato.
3. Close the lid and cook the dip on low for 5 hours.

Nutrition Info:
- Per Serving: 156 calories, 8.7g protein, 22.5g carbohydrates, 5.2g fat, 8.3g fiber, 11mg cholesterol, 140mg sodium, 575mg potassium.

Squash Noodles

Servings:4 | Cooking Time: 4 Hours

Ingredients:
- 1-pound butternut squash, seeded, halved
- 1 tablespoon vegan butter
- 1 teaspoon salt
- ½ teaspoon garlic powder
- 3 cups of water

Directions:
1. Pour water in the Crock Pot.
2. Add butternut squash and close the lid.
3. Cook the vegetable on high for 4 hours.
4. Then drain water and shred the squash flesh with the help of the fork and transfer in the bowl.
5. Add garlic powder, salt, and butter. Mix the squash noodles.

Nutrition Info:
- Per Serving: 78 calories, 1.2g protein, 13.5g carbohydrates, 3g fat, 2.3g fiber, 8mg cholesterol, 612mg sodium, 406mg potassium

Apples Sauté

Servings:4 | Cooking Time: 2 Hours

Ingredients:
- 4 cups apples, chopped
- 1 cup of water
- 1 teaspoon ground cinnamon
- 1 teaspoon sugar

Directions:
1. Put all ingredients in the Crock Pot.
2. Cook the apple sauté for 2 hours on High.
3. When the meal is cooked, let it cool until warm.

Nutrition Info:
- Per Serving: 121 calories, 0.6g protein, 32.3g carbohydrates, 0.4g fat, 5.7g fiber, 0mg cholesterol, 4mg sodium, 242mg potassium.

Garlic Asparagus

Servings:5 | Cooking Time: 6 Hours

Ingredients:
- 1-pound asparagus, trimmed
- 1 teaspoon salt
- 1 teaspoon garlic powder
- 1 tablespoon vegan butter

- 1 ½ cup vegetable stock

Directions:
1. Chop the asparagus roughly and sprinkle with salt and garlic powder.
2. Put the vegetables in the Crock Pot.
3. Add vegan butter and vegetable stock. Close the lid.
4. Cook the asparagus on Low for 6 hours.

Nutrition Info:
- Per Serving: 33 calories, 2.3g protein, 6.1g carbohydrates, 1g fat, 2g fiber, 0mg cholesterol, 687mg sodium, 190mg potassium.

Cream Zucchini Pasta

Servings:2 | Cooking Time: 2 Hours

Ingredients:
- 2 large zucchinis, trimmed
- 1 cup coconut cream
- 1 teaspoon white pepper
- 2 oz vegan Parmesan, grated

Directions:
1. Make the strips from zucchini with the help of a spiralizer and put in the Crock Pot.
2. Add white pepper and coconut cream.
3. Then top the zucchini with grated vegan Parmesan and close the lid.
4. Cook the meal on low for 2 hours.

Nutrition Info:
- Per Serving: 223 calories, 14.1g protein, 16.3g carbohydrates, 13.4g fat, 3.8g fiber, 43mg cholesterol, 335mg sodium, 904mg potassium.

Eggplant Parmesan Casserole

Servings:3 | Cooking Time: 3 Hours

Ingredients:
- 1 medium eggplant, sliced
- 1 large egg
- Salt and pepper to taste
- 1 cup almond flour
- 1 cup parmesan cheese

Directions:
1. Place the eggplant slices in the crockpot.
2. Pour in the eggs and season with salt and pepper.
3. Stir in the almond flour and sprinkle with parmesan cheese.

4. Stir to combine everything.
5. Close the lid and cook on low for 3 hours or on high for 2 hours.

Nutrition Info:
- Calories per serving: 212; Carbohydrates: 17g; Protein: 15g; Fat:12.1 g; Sugar: 1.2g; Sodium: 231mg; Fiber:8.1 g

Vegetarian Red Coconut Curry

Servings:4 | Cooking Time: 3 Hours

Ingredients:
- 1 cup broccoli florets
- 1 large handful spinach, rinsed
- 1 tablespoon red curry paste
- 1 cup coconut cream
- 1 teaspoon garlic, minced

Directions:
1. Combine all ingredients in the crockpot.
2. Close the lid and cook on low for 3 hours or on high for 1 hour.

Nutrition Info:
- Calories per serving: 226; Carbohydrates: 8g; Protein: 5.2g; Fat:21.4 g; Sugar: 0.4g; Sodium: 341mg; Fiber:4.3 g

Lazy Minestrone Soup

Servings:4 | Cooking Time: 3 Hours

Ingredients:
- 1 cup zucchini, sliced
- 2 cups chicken broth
- 1 package diced vegetables of your choice
- 2 tablespoons basil, chopped
- ½ cup diced celery

Directions:
1. Place all ingredients in the crockpot.
2. Season with salt and pepper to taste.
3. Close the lid and cook on low for 3 hours or on high for 1 hour.

Nutrition Info:
- Calories per serving: 259; Carbohydrates: 13.5g; Protein:30.3 g; Fat: 8.3g; Sugar: 0.4g; Sodium: 643mg; Fiber: 4.2g

Butter Hasselback Potatoes

Servings:2 | Cooking Time: 4 Hours

Ingredients:
- 2 large Russet potatoes
- 1 tablespoon olive oil
- 2 teaspoons vegan butter
- 1 teaspoon onion powder
- ½ cup vegetable stock

Directions:
1. Cut the potatoes in the shape of Hasselback and place it in the Crock Pot.
2. Sprinkle them with olive oil, butter, and onion powder.
3. Add vegetable stock and close the lid.
4. Cook the potatoes on High for 4 hours or until they are soft.

Nutrition Info:
- Per Serving: 355 calories, 6.5g protein, 59.1g carbohydrates, 11.3g fat, 8.9g fiber, 10mg cholesterol, 241mg sodium, 1518mg potassium.

Zucchini Mash

Servings:2 | Cooking Time: 45 Minutes

Ingredients:
- 2 cups zucchini, grated
- 1 tablespoon olive oil
- ¼ cup of water
- ½ teaspoon ground black pepper
- 2 tablespoons sour cream

Directions:
1. Put all ingredients in the Crock Pot and gently stir.
2. Cook the zucchini mash on High for 45 minutes.

Nutrition Info:
- Per Serving: 105 calories, 1.8g protein, 4.6g carbohydrates, 9.7g fat, 1.4g fiber, 5mg cholesterol, 19mg sodium, 320mg potassium.

Paprika Baby Carrot

Servings:2 | Cooking Time: 2.5 Hours

Ingredients:
- 1 tablespoon ground paprika
- 2 cups baby carrot
- 1 teaspoon cumin seeds
- 1 cup of water
- 1 teaspoon vegan butter

Directions:
1. Pour water in the Crock Pot.
2. Add baby carrot, cumin seeds, and ground paprika.
3. Close the lid and cook the carrot on High for 2.5 hours.
4. Then drain water, add butter, and shake the vegetables.

Nutrition Info:
- Per Serving: 60 calories, 1.6g protein, 8.6g carbohydrates, 2.7g fat, 4.2g fiber, 5mg cholesterol, 64mg sodium, 220mg potassium.

Thyme Fennel Bulb

Servings:4 | Cooking Time: 3 Hours

Ingredients:
- 16 oz fennel bulb
- 1 tablespoon thyme
- 1 cup of water
- 1 teaspoon salt
- 1 teaspoon peppercorns

Directions:
1. Chop the fennel bulb roughly and put it in the Crock Pot.
2. Add thyme, water, salt, and peppercorns.
3. Cook the fennel on High for 3 hours.
4. Then drain water, remove peppercorns, and transfer the fennel in the serving plates.

Nutrition Info:
- Per Serving: 38 calories, 1.5g protein, 9g carbohydrates, 0.3g fat, 3.9g fiber, 0mg cholesterol, 643mg sodium, 482mg potassium.

Curry Couscous

Servings:4 | Cooking Time: 20 Minutes

Ingredients:
- 1 cup of water
- 1 cup couscous
- ½ cup coconut cream
- 1 teaspoon salt

Directions:
1. Put all ingredients in the Crock Pot and close the lid.
2. Cook the couscous on High for 20 minutes.

Nutrition Info:
- Per Serving: 182 calories, 5.8g protein, 34.4g carbohydrates, 2g fat, 2.2g fiber, 6mg cholesterol, 597mg sodium, 84mg potassium.

Spicy Eggplant With Red Pepper And Parsley

Servings:4 | Cooking Time: 3 Hours

Ingredients:
- 1 large eggplant, sliced
- 2 tablespoons parsley, chopped
- 1 big red bell pepper, chopped
- Salt and pepper to taste
- 2 tablespoons balsamic vinegar

Directions:
1. Place all ingredients in a mixing bowl.
2. Toss to coat ingredients.
3. Place in the crockpot and cook on low for 3 hours or on high for 1 hour.

Nutrition Info:
- Calories per serving: 52; Carbohydrates:11.67 g; Protein:1.8 g; Fat:0.31 g; Sugar: 0.2g; Sodium: 142mg; Fiber: 9.4g

Baked Onions

Servings:4 | Cooking Time: 2 Hours

Ingredients:
- 4 onions, peeled
- 1 tablespoon coconut oil
- 1 teaspoon salt
- 1 teaspoon brown sugar
- 1 cup coconut cream

Directions:
1. Put coconut oil in the Crock Pot.
2. Then make the small cuts in the onions with the help of the knife and put in the Crock Pot in one layer.
3. Sprinkle the vegetables with salt, and brown sugar.
4. Add coconut cream and close the lid.
5. Cook the onions on High for 2 hours.

Nutrition Info:
- Per Serving: 214 calories, 2.6g protein, 14.3g carbohydrates, 17.8g fat, 3.7g fiber, 0mg cholesterol, 595mg sodium, 320mg potassium.

Sugar Yams

Servings:4 | Cooking Time: 2 Hours

Ingredients:
- 4 yams, peeled
- 1 cup of water
- 1 tablespoon sugar
- 2 tablespoons vegan butter

Directions:
1. Cut the yams into halves and put them in the Crock Pot.
2. Add water and cook for 2 hours on high.
3. Then melt the butter in the skillet.
4. Add sugar and heat it until sugar is melted.
5. Then drain water from the yams.
6. Put the yams in the sugar butter and roast for 2 minutes per side.

Nutrition Info:
- Per Serving: 63 calories, 0.1g protein, 3.3g carbohydrates, 5.8g fat, 0g fiber, 15mg cholesterol, 43mg sodium, 9mg potassium.

Artichoke Dip

Servings:6 | Cooking Time: 6 Hours

Ingredients:
- 2 cups Cheddar cheese, shredded
- 1 cup of coconut milk
- 1-pound artichoke, drained, chopped
- 1 tablespoon Ranch dressing

Directions:
1. Put all ingredients in the Crock Pot.
2. Mix them gently and close the lid.
3. Cook the artichoke dip on Low for 6 hours.

Nutrition Info:

- Per Serving: 280 calories, 12.8g protein, 10.8g carbohydrates, 22.1g fat, 5g fiber, 40mg cholesterol, 325mg sodium, 422mg potassium.

Paprika Okra

Servings:4 | Cooking Time: 40 Minutes

Ingredients:
- 4 cups okra, sliced
- 1 tablespoon smoked paprika
- 1 teaspoon salt
- 2 tablespoons coconut oil
- 1 cup organic almond milk

Directions:
1. Pour almond milk in the Crock Pot.
2. Add coconut oil, salt, and smoked paprika.
3. Then add sliced okra and gently mix the ingredients.
4. Cook the okra on High for 40 minutes. Then cooked okra should be tender but not soft.

Nutrition Info:
- Per Serving: 119 calories, 2.4g protein, 10.4g carbohydrates, 7.8g fat, 3.9g fiber, 0mg cholesterol, 624mg sodium, 340mg potassium.

Corn Pudding

Servings:4 | Cooking Time: 5 Hours

Ingredients:
- 3 cups corn kernels
- 2 cups heavy cream
- 3 tablespoons muffin mix
- 1 oz Parmesan, grated

Directions:
1. Mix heavy cream with muffin mix and pour the liquid in the Crock Pot.
2. Add corn kernels and Parmesan. Stir the mixture well.
3. Close the lid and cook the pudding on Low for 5 hours.

Nutrition Info:
- Per Serving: 371 calories, 21.8g protein, 31.4g carbohydrates, 26.3g fat, 3.2g fiber, 87mg cholesterol, 180mg sodium, 378mg potassium.

Braised Sesame Spinach

Servings:4 | Cooking Time: 35 Minutes

Ingredients:
- 1 tablespoon sesame seeds
- ¼ cup of soy sauce
- 2 tablespoons sesame oil
- 4 cups spinach, chopped
- 1 cup of water

Directions:
1. Pour water in the Crock Pot.
2. Add spinach and cook it on High for 35 minutes.
3. After this, drain water and transfer the spinach in the big bowl.
4. Add soy sauce, sesame oil, and sesame seeds.
5. Carefully mix the spinach and transfer in the serving plates/bowls.

Nutrition Info:
- Per Serving: 88 calories, 2.3g protein, 2.8g carbohydrates, 8.1g fat, 1.1g fiber, 2.8mg cholesterol, 924mg sodium, 213mg potassium.

Split Pea Paste

Servings:4 | Cooking Time: 2 Hours

Ingredients:
- 2 cups split peas
- 2 cups of water
- 1 tablespoon coconut oil
- 1 teaspoon salt
- 1 teaspoon ground black pepper

Directions:
1. Pour water in the Crock Pot.
2. Add split peas and close the lid.
3. Cook them for 2 hours on high or until they are soft.
4. Then drain water and transfer the split peas in the food processor.
5. Add coconut oil, salt, and ground black pepper.
6. Blend the mixture until smooth.

Nutrition Info:
- Per Serving: 367 calories, 24.2g protein, 59.8g carbohydrates, 4.6g fat, 25.3g fiber, 0mg cholesterol, 600mg sodium, 974mg potassium.

Creamy White Mushrooms

Servings:4 | Cooking Time: 8 Hours

Ingredients:
- 1-pound white mushrooms, chopped
- 1 cup cream
- 1 teaspoon chili flakes
- 1 teaspoon ground black pepper
- 1 tablespoon dried parsley

Directions:
1. Put all ingredients in the Crock Pot.
2. Cook the mushrooms on low for 8 hours.
3. When the mushrooms are cooked, transfer them in the serving bowls and cool for 10-15 minutes.

Nutrition Info:
- Per Serving: 65 calories, 4.1g protein, 6g carbohydrates, 3.7g fat, 1.3g fiber, 11mg cholesterol, 27mg sodium, 396mg potassium.

Vegetarian Keto Burgers

Servings:4 | Cooking Time: 4 Hours

Ingredients:
- 2 Portobello mushrooms, chopped
- 2 tablespoons basil, chopped
- 1 clove of garlic, minced
- 1 egg, beaten
- ½ cup boiled cauliflower, mashed

Directions:
1. Line the bottom of the crockpot with foil.
2. In a food processor, combine all ingredients.
3. Make 4 burger patties using your hands and place gently in the crockpot.
4. Close the lid and cook on low for 4 hours or on high for 3 hours.

Nutrition Info:
- Calories per serving: 134; Carbohydrates: 18g; Protein: 10g; Fat: 3.1g; Sugar:0.9g; Sodium:235mg; Fiber: 5g

Brussel Sprouts

Servings:4 | Cooking Time: 2.5 Hours

Ingredients:
- 1-pound Brussel sprouts
- 2 oz tofu, chopped, cooked
- 1 teaspoon cayenne pepper
- 2 cups of water
- 1 tablespoon vegan butter

Directions:
1. Pour water in the Crock Pot.
2. Add Brussel sprouts and cayenne pepper.
3. Cook the vegetables on high for 2.5 hours.
4. Then drain water and mix Brussel sprouts with butter and tofu.
5. Shake the vegetables gently.

Nutrition Info:
- Per Serving: 153 calories, 9.2g protein, 10.8g carbohydrates, 9.3g fat, 4.4g fiber, 23mg cholesterol, 380mg sodium, 532mg potassium

Sweet Potato Puree

Servings:2 | Cooking Time: 4 Hours

Ingredients:
- 2 cups sweet potato, chopped
- 1 cup of water
- ¼ cup half and half
- 1 oz scallions, chopped
- 1 teaspoon salt

Directions:
1. Put sweet potatoes in the Crock Pot.
2. Add water and salt.
3. Cook them on High for 4 hours.
4. The drain water and transfer the sweet potatoes in the food processor.
5. Add half and half and blend until smooth.
6. Transfer the puree in the bowl, and scallions, and mix carefully.

Nutrition Info:
- Per Serving: 225 calories, 5.2g protein, 43.7g carbohydrates, 3.9g fat, 7g fiber, 11mg cholesterol, 1253mg sodium, 1030mg potassium.

Cauliflower Curry

Servings:4 | Cooking Time: 2 Hours

Ingredients:
- 4 cups cauliflower
- 1 tablespoon curry paste
- 2 cups of coconut milk

Directions:
1. In the mixing bowl mix coconut milk with curry paste until smooth.
2. Put cauliflower in the Crock Pot.
3. Pour the curry liquid over the cauliflower and close the lid.
4. Cook the meal on High for 2 hours.

Nutrition Info:
- Per Serving: 236 calories, 4.9g protein, 13g carbohydrates, 30.9g fat, 5.1g fiber, 0mg cholesterol, 48mg sodium, 619mg potassium.

Coconut Milk Lentils Bowl

Servings:5 | Cooking Time: 9 Hours

Ingredients:
- 2 cups brown lentils
- 3 cups of coconut milk
- 3 cups of water
- 1 teaspoon ground nutmeg
- 1 teaspoon salt

Directions:
1. Mix the brown lentils with salt and ground nutmeg and put in the Crock Pot.
2. Add coconut milk and water.
3. Close the lid and cook the lentils on Low for 9 hours.

Nutrition Info:
- Per Serving: 364 calories, 5.3g protein, 12.1g carbohydrates, 34.7g fat, 4.9g fiber, 0mg cholesterol, 491mg sodium, 382mg potassium.

Sesame Asparagus

Servings:4 | Cooking Time: 3 Hours

Ingredients:
- 1-pound asparagus
- ½ cup of soy sauce
- ½ cup vegetable stock
- 1 teaspoon sesame seeds

- 1 tablespoon vegan butter

Directions:
1. Trim the asparagus and put it in the Crock Pot.
2. Add soy sauce and vegetable stock.
3. Then add sesame seeds and butter.
4. Close the lid and cook the meal on High for 3 hours.

Nutrition Info:
- Per Serving: 71 calories, 4.7g protein, 7.1g carbohydrates, 3.5g fat, 2.7g fiber, 8mg cholesterol, 1915mg sodium, 304mg potassium.

Egg Cauliflower

Servings:2 | Cooking Time: 4 Hours

Ingredients:
- 2 cups cauliflower, shredded
- 4 eggs, beaten
- 1 tablespoon vegan butter
- ½ teaspoon salt

Directions:
1. Mix eggs with salt.
2. Put the shredded cauliflower in the Crock Pot.
3. Add eggs and vegan butter. Gently mix the mixture.
4. Close the lid and cook the meal on low for 4 hours. Stir the cauliflower with the help of the fork every 1 hour.

Nutrition Info:
- Per Serving: 176 calories, 13.5g protein, 9.9g carbohydrates, 9.7g fat, 2.6g fiber, 372mg cholesterol, 746mg sodium, 421mg potassium.

Spinach With Halloumi Cheese Casserole

Servings:4 | Cooking Time: 2 Hours

Ingredients:
- 1 package spinach, rinsed
- ½ cup walnuts, chopped
- Salt and pepper to taste
- 1 tablespoon balsamic vinegar
- 1 ½ cups halloumi cheese, grated

Directions:
1. Place spinach and walnuts in the crockpot.
2. Season with salt and pepper. Drizzle with balsamic vinegar.
3. Top with halloumi cheese and cook on low for 2

hours or on high for 30 minutes

Nutrition Info:
- Calories per serving: 560; Carbohydrates: 7g; Protein:21 g; Fat: 47g; Sugar:2.1 g; Sodium: 231mg; Fiber:3 g

Miso Asparagus

Servings:2 | Cooking Time: 2.5 Hours

Ingredients:
- 1 teaspoon miso paste
- 1 cup of water
- 1 tablespoon fish sauce
- 10 oz asparagus, chopped
- 1 teaspoon avocado oil

Directions:
1. Mix miso paste with water and pour in the Crock Pot.
2. Add fish sauce, asparagus, and avocado oil.
3. Close the lid and cook the meal on High for 2.5 hours.

Nutrition Info:
- Per Serving: 40 calories, 3.9g protein, 6.7g carbohydrates, 0.6g fat, 3.2g fiber, 0mg cholesterol, 808mg sodium, 327mg potassium.

Broccoli And Cheese Casserole

Servings:4 | Cooking Time: 4 Hours

Ingredients:
- ¾ cup almond flour
- 1 head of broccoli, cut into florets
- 2 large eggs, beaten
- Salt and pepper to taste
- ½ cup mozzarella cheese

Directions:
1. Place the almond flour and broccoli in the crockpot.
2. Stir in the eggs and season with salt and pepper to taste.
3. Sprinkle with mozzarella cheese.
4. Close the lid and cook on low for 4 hours or on high for 2 hours.

Nutrition Info:
- Calories per serving: 78; Carbohydrates: 4g; Protein: 8.2g; Fat:5.8 g; Sugar: 0g; Sodium: 231mg; Fiber:2.3 g

Masala Eggplants

Servings:2 | Cooking Time: 2 Hours

Ingredients:
- ½ cup coconut cream
- ½ cup of water
- 1 teaspoon garam masala
- 2 eggplants, chopped
- 1 teaspoon salt

Directions:
1. Sprinkle the eggplants with salt and leave for 10 minutes.
2. Then drain eggplant juice and transfer the vegetables in the Crock Pot.
3. Add garam masala, water, and coconut cream.
4. Cook the meal on High for 2 hours.

Nutrition Info:
- Per Serving: 275 calories, 6.8g protein, 35.5g carbohydrates, 15.3g fat, 20.7g fiber, 0mg cholesterol, 1186mg sodium, 1414mg potassium.

Cream Of Mushroom Soup

Servings:4 | Cooking Time: 3 Hours

Ingredients:
- 1 tablespoons olive oil
- ½ cup onion, diced
- 20 ounces mushrooms, sliced
- 2 cups chicken broth
- 1 cup heavy cream

Directions:
1. In a skillet, heat the oil over medium flame and sauté the onions until translucent or slightly brown on the edges.
2. Transfer into the crockpot and add the mushrooms and chicken broth. Season with salt and pepper to taste.
3. Close the lid and cook on low for 6 hours or on high for 3 hours until the mushrooms are soft
4. Halfway before the cooking time ends, stir in the heavy cream.

Nutrition Info:
- Calories per serving: 229; Carbohydrates: 9g; Protein: 5g; Fat: 21g; Sugar:3 g; Sodium:214 mg; Fiber: 2g

Buffalo Cremini Mushrooms

Servings:4 | Cooking Time: 6 Hours

Ingredients:
- 3 cups cremini mushrooms, trimmed
- 2 oz buffalo sauce
- ½ cup of water
- 2 tablespoons coconut oil

Directions:
1. Pour water in the Crock Pot.
2. Melt the coconut oil in the skillet.
3. Add mushrooms and roast them for 3-4 minutes per side. Transfer the roasted mushrooms in the Crock Pot.
4. Cook them on Low for 4 hours.
5. Then add buffalo sauce and carefully mix.
6. Cook the mushrooms for 2 hours on low.

Nutrition Info:
- Per Serving: 79 calories, 1.4g protein, 3.2g carbohydrates, 6.9g fat, 0.8g fiber, 0mg cholesterol, 458mg sodium, 242mg potassium.

Sautéed Greens

Servings:4 | Cooking Time: 1 Hour

Ingredients:
- 1 cup spinach, chopped
- 2 cups collard greens, chopped
- 1 cup Swiss chard, chopped
- 2 cups of water
- ½ cup half and half

Directions:
1. Put spinach, collard greens, and Swiss chard in the Crock Pot.
2. Add water and close the lid.
3. Cook the greens on High for 1 hour.
4. Then drain water and transfer the greens in the bowl.
5. Bring the half and half to boil and pour over greens.
6. Carefully mix the greens.

Nutrition Info:
- Per Serving: 49 calories, 1.8g protein, 3.2g carbohydrates, 3.7g fat, 1.1g fiber, 11mg cholesterol, 45mg sodium, 117mg potassium.

Coconut Cauliflower Florets

Servings:4 | Cooking Time: 4 Hours

Ingredients:
- 2 cups cauliflower, florets
- 1 cup of coconut milk
- 1 tablespoon coconut flakes
- 1 teaspoon salt
- 1 teaspoon ground turmeric

Directions:
1. Sprinkle the cauliflower florets with ground turmeric and salt, and transfer in the Crock Pot.
2. Add coconut flakes and coconut milk.
3. Close the lid and cook the meal on Low for 4 hours.
4. Carefully mix the cauliflower before serving.

Nutrition Info:
- Per Serving: 157 calories, 24.g protein, 6.5g carbohydrates, 14.8g fat, 2.8g fiber, 0mg cholesterol, 606mg sodium, 328mg potassium.

Hot Tofu

Servings:4 | Cooking Time: 4 Hours

Ingredients:
- 1-pound firm tofu, cubed
- 1 tablespoon hot sauce
- ½ cup vegetable stock
- 1 teaspoon miso paste

Directions:
1. Mix vegetables tock with miso paste and pour in the Crock Pot.
2. Add hot sauce and tofu.
3. Close the lid and cook the meal on Low for 4 hours.
4. Then transfer the tofu and liquid in the serving bowls.

Nutrition Info:
- Per Serving: 83 calories, 9.5g protein, 2.5g carbohydrates, 4.8g fat, 1.2g fiber, 0mg cholesterol, 168mg sodium, 176mg potassium.

Sauteed Spinach

Servings:3 | Cooking Time: 1 Hour

Ingredients:
- 3 cups spinach
- 1 tablespoon vegan butter, softened
- 2 cups of water
- 2 oz Parmesan, grated
- 1 teaspoon pine nuts, crushed

Directions:
1. Chop the spinach and put it in the Crock Pot.
2. Add water and close the lid.
3. Cook the spinach on High for 1 hour.
4. Then drain water and put the cooked spinach in the bowl.
5. Add pine nuts, Parmesan, and butter.
6. Carefully mix the spinach.

Nutrition Info:
- Per Serving: 108 calories, 7.1g protein, 1.9g carbohydrates, 8.7g fat, 0.7g fiber, 24mg cholesterol, 231mg sodium, 176mg potassium.

Butter Asparagus

Servings:4 | Cooking Time: 5 Hours

Ingredients:
- 1-pound asparagus
- 2 tablespoons vegan butter
- 1 teaspoon ground black pepper
- 1 cup vegetable stock

Directions:
1. Pour the vegetable stock in the Crock Pot.
2. Chop the asparagus roughly and add in the Crock Pot.
3. Close the lid and cook the asparagus for 5 hours on Low.
4. Then drain water and transfer the asparagus in the bowl.
5. Sprinkle it with ground black pepper and butter.

Nutrition Info:
- Per Serving: 77 calories, 2.8g protein, 4.9g carbohydrates, 6.1g fat, 2.5g fiber, 15mg cholesterol, 234mg sodium, 241mg potassium.

Asian Broccoli Sauté

Servings:4 | Cooking Time: 3 Hours

Ingredients:
- 1 tablespoon coconut oil
- 1 head broccoli, cut into florets
- 1 tablespoon coconut aminos or soy sauce
- 1 teaspoon ginger, grated
- Salt and pepper to taste

Directions:
1. Place the ingredients in the crockpot.
2. Toss everything to combine.
3. Close the lid and cook on low for 3 hours or on high for an hour.
4. Once cooked, sprinkle with sesame seeds or sesame oil.

Nutrition Info:
- Calories per serving: 62; Carbohydrates:3.6 g; Protein: 1.8g; Fat: 4.3g; Sugar:0.3 g; Sodium: 87mg; Fiber: 2.1g

Chapter 9 Side Dish Recipes

Chapter 9 Side Dish Recipes

Mango Rice

Servings: 2 | Cooking Time: 2 Hours

Ingredients:
- 1 cup rice
- 2 cups chicken stock
- ½ cup mango, peeled and cubed
- Salt and black pepper to the taste
- 1 teaspoon olive oil

Directions:
1. In your Crock Pot, mix the rice with the stock and the other ingredients, toss, put the lid on and cook on High for 2 hours.
2. Divide between plates and serve as a side dish.

Nutrition Info:
- calories 152, fat 4, fiber 5, carbs 18, protein 4

Rosemary Potatoes

Servings: 12 | Cooking Time: 3 Hours

Ingredients:
- 2 tablespoons olive oil
- 3 pounds new potatoes, halved
- 7 garlic cloves, minced
- 1 tablespoon rosemary, chopped
- A pinch of salt and black pepper

Directions:
1. In your Crock Pot, mix oil with potatoes, garlic, rosemary, salt and pepper, toss, cover and cook on High for 3 hours.
2. Divide between plates and serve as a side dish.

Nutrition Info:
- calories 102, fat 2, fiber 2, carbs 18, protein 2

Buttery Mushrooms

Servings: 6 | Cooking Time: 4 Hours

Ingredients:
- 1 yellow onion, chopped
- 1 pounds mushrooms, halved
- ½ cup butter, melted
- 1 teaspoon Italian seasoning
- Salt and black pepper to the taste
- 1 teaspoon sweet paprika

Directions:
1. In your Crock Pot, mix mushrooms with onion, butter, Italian seasoning, salt, pepper and paprika, toss, cover and cook on Low for 4 hours.
2. Divide between plates and serve as a side dish.

Nutrition Info:
- calories 120, fat 6, fiber 1, carbs 8, protein 4

Beets And Carrots

Servings: 8 | Cooking Time: 7 Hours

Ingredients:
- 2 tablespoons stevia
- ¾ cup pomegranate juice
- 2 teaspoons ginger, grated
- 2 and ½ pounds beets, peeled and cut into wedges
- 12 ounces carrots, cut into medium wedges

Directions:
1. In your Crock Pot, mix beets with carrots, ginger, stevia and pomegranate juice, toss, cover and cook on Low for 7 hours.
2. Divide between plates and serve as a side dish.

Nutrition Info:
- calories 125, fat 0, fiber 4, carbs 28, protein 3

Maple Sweet Potatoes

Servings: 10 | Cooking Time: 5 Hours

Ingredients:
- 8 sweet potatoes, halved and sliced
- 1 cup walnuts, chopped
- ½ cup cherries, dried and chopped
- ½ cup maple syrup
- ¼ cup apple juice
- A pinch of salt

Directions:
1. Arrange sweet potatoes in your Crock Pot, add walnuts, dried cherries, maple syrup, apple juice and a pinch of salt, toss a bit, cover and cook on Low for 5 hours.
2. Divide between plates and serve as a side dish.

Nutrition Info:
- calories 271, fat 6, fiber 4, carbs 26, protein 6

Sage Sweet Potatoes

Servings: 2 | Cooking Time: 3 Hours

Ingredients:
- ½ pound sweet potatoes, thinly sliced
- 1 tablespoon sage, chopped
- 2 tablespoons orange juice
- A pinch of salt and black pepper
- ½ cup veggie stock
- ½ tablespoon olive oil

Directions:
1. In your Crock Pot, mix the potatoes with the sage and the other ingredients, toss, put the lid on and cook on High for 3 hours.
2. Divide between plates and serve as a side dish.

Nutrition Info:
- calories 189, fat 4, fiber 4, carbs 17, protein 4

Beans And Red Peppers

Servings: 2 | Cooking Time: 2 Hrs.

Ingredients:
- 2 cups green beans, halved
- 1 red bell pepper, cut into strips
- Salt and black pepper to the taste
- 1 tbsp olive oil
- 1 and ½ tbsp honey mustard

Directions:
1. Add green beans, honey mustard, red bell pepper, oil, salt, and black to Crock Pot.
2. Put the cooker's lid on and set the cooking time to 2 hours on High settings.
3. Serve warm.

Nutrition Info:
- Per Serving: Calories: 50, Total Fat: 0g, Fiber: 4g, Total Carbs: 8g, Protein: 2g

Pink Rice

Servings: 8 | Cooking Time: 5 Hours

Ingredients:
- 1 teaspoon salt
- 2 and ½ cups water
- 2 cups pink rice

Directions:
1. Put the rice in your Crock Pot add water and salt, stir, cover and cook on Low for 5 hours
2. Stir rice a bit, divide it between plates and serve as a side dish.

Nutrition Info:
- calories 120, fat 3, fiber 3, carbs 16, protein 4

Green Beans And Red Peppers

Servings: 2 | Cooking Time: 2 Hours

Ingredients:
- 2 cups green beans, halved
- 1 red bell pepper, cut into strips
- Salt and black pepper to the taste
- 1 tablespoon olive oil
- 1 and ½ tablespoon honey mustard

Directions:
1. In your Crock Pot, mix green beans with bell pepper, salt, pepper, oil and honey mustard, toss, cover and cook on High for 2 hours.
2. Divide between plates and serve as a side dish.

Nutrition Info:
- calories 50, fat 0, fiber 4, carbs 8, protein 2

Cumin Quinoa Pilaf

Servings: 2 | Cooking Time: 2 Hours

Ingredients:
- 1 cup quinoa
- 2 teaspoons butter, melted
- Salt and black pepper to the taste
- 1 teaspoon turmeric powder
- 2 cups chicken stock
- 1 teaspoon cumin, ground

Directions:
1. Grease your Crock Pot with the butter, add the quinoa and the other ingredients, toss, put the lid on and cook on High for 2 hours
2. Divide between plates and serve as a side dish.

Nutrition Info:
- calories 152, fat 3, fiber 6, carbs 8, protein 4

Chicken With Sweet Potato

Servings: 6 | Cooking Time: 3 Hours

Ingredients:
- 16 oz. sweet potato, peeled and diced
- 3 cups chicken stock
- 1 tbsp salt
- 3 tbsp margarine
- 2 tbsp cream cheese

Directions:
1. Add sweet potato, chicken stock, and salt to the Crock Pot.
2. Put the cooker's lid on and set the cooking time to 5 hours on High settings.
3. Drain the slow-cooked potatoes and transfer them to a suitable bowl.
4. Mash the sweet potatoes and stir in cream cheese and margarine.
5. Serve fresh.

Nutrition Info:
- Per Serving: Calories: 472, Total Fat: 31.9g, Fiber: 6.7g, Total Carbs: 43.55g, Protein: 3g

Mexican Avocado Rice

Servings: 8 | Cooking Time: 4 Hrs

Ingredients:
- 1 cup long-grain rice
- 1 and ¼ cups veggie stock
- ½ cup cilantro, chopped
- ½ avocado, pitted, peeled and chopped
- Salt and black pepper to the taste
- ¼ cup green hot sauce

Directions:
1. Add rice and stock to the Crock Pot.
2. Put the cooker's lid on and set the cooking time to 4 hours on Low settings.
3. Meanwhile, blend avocado flesh with hot sauce, cilantro, salt, and black pepper.
4. Serve the cooked rice with avocado sauce on top.

Nutrition Info:
- Per Serving: Calories: 100, Total Fat: 3g, Fiber: 6g, Total Carbs: 18g, Protein: 4g

Italian Eggplant

Servings: 2 | Cooking Time: 2 Hours

Ingredients:
- 2 small eggplants, roughly cubed
- ½ cup heavy cream
- Salt and black pepper to the taste
- 1 tablespoon olive oil
- A pinch of hot pepper flakes
- 2 tablespoons oregano, chopped

Directions:
1. In your Crock Pot, mix the eggplants with the cream and the other ingredients, toss, put the lid on and cook on High for 2 hours.
2. Divide between plates and serve as a side dish.

Nutrition Info:
- calories 132, fat 4, fiber 6, carbs 12, protein 3

Garlicky Black Beans

Servings: 8 | Cooking Time: 7 Hours

Ingredients:
- 1 cup black beans, soaked overnight, drained and rinsed
- 1 cup of water
- Salt and black pepper to the taste
- 1 spring onion, chopped
- 2 garlic cloves, minced
- ½ tsp cumin seeds

Directions:
1. Add beans, salt, black pepper, cumin seeds, garlic, and onion to the Crock Pot.
2. Put the cooker's lid on and set the cooking time to 7 hours on Low settings.
3. Serve warm.

Nutrition Info:
- Per Serving: Calories: 300, Total Fat: 4g, Fiber: 6g, Total Carbs: 20g, Protein: 15g

Lemon Artichokes

Servings: 2 | Cooking Time: 3 Hours

Ingredients:
- 1 cup veggie stock
- 2 medium artichokes, trimmed
- 1 tablespoon lemon juice
- 1 tablespoon lemon zest, grated
- Salt to the taste

Directions:
1. In your Crock Pot, mix the artichokes with the stock and the other ingredients, toss, put the lid on and cook on Low for 3 hours.
2. Divide artichokes between plates and serve as a side dish.

Nutrition Info:
- calories 100, fat 2, fiber 5, carbs 10, protein 4

Mexican Rice

Servings: 8 | Cooking Time: 4 Hours

Ingredients:
- 1 cup long grain rice
- 1 and ¼ cups veggie stock
- ½ cup cilantro, chopped
- ½ avocado, pitted, peeled and chopped
- Salt and black pepper to the taste
- ¼ cup green hot sauce

Directions:
1. Put the rice in your Crock Pot, add stock, stir, cover, cook on Low for 4 hours, fluff with a fork and transfer to a bowl.
2. In your food processor, mix avocado with hot sauce and cilantro, blend well, pour over rice, toss well, add salt and pepper, divide between plates and serve as a side dish.

Nutrition Info:
- calories 100, fat 3, fiber 6, carbs 18, protein 4

Rosemary Leeks

Servings: 2 | Cooking Time: 3 Hours

Ingredients:
- ½ tablespoon olive oil
- ½ leeks, sliced
- ½ cup tomato sauce
- 2 garlic cloves, minced
- Salt and black pepper to the taste
- ¼ tablespoon rosemary, chopped

Directions:
1. In your Crock Pot, mix the leeks with the oil, sauce and the other ingredients, toss, put the lid on, cook on High for 3 hours, divide between plates and serve as a side dish.

Nutrition Info:
- calories 202, fat 2, fiber 6, carbs 18, protein 8

Okra Mix

Servings: 4 | Cooking Time: 8 Hours

Ingredients:
- 2 garlic cloves, minced
- 1 yellow onion, chopped
- 14 ounces tomato sauce
- 1 teaspoon sweet paprika
- 2 cups okra, sliced
- Salt and black pepper to the taste

Directions:
1. In your Crock Pot, mix garlic with the onion, tomato sauce, paprika, okra, salt and pepper, cover and cook on Low for 8 hours.
2. Divide between plates and serve as a side dish.

Nutrition Info:
- calories 200, fat 6, fiber 5, carbs 10, protein 4

Roasted Beets

Servings: 5 | Cooking Time: 4 Hours

Ingredients:
- 10 small beets
- 5 teaspoons olive oil
- A pinch of salt and black pepper

Directions:
1. Divide each beet on a tin foil piece, drizzle oil, season them with salt and pepper, rub well, wrap beets, place them in your Crock Pot, cover and cook on High for 4 hours.
2. Unwrap beets, cool them down a bit, peel, slice and serve them as a side dish.

Nutrition Info:
- calories 100, fat 2, fiber 2, carbs 4, protein 5

Orange Carrots Mix

Servings: 2 | Cooking Time: 6 Hours

Ingredients:
- ½ pound carrots, sliced
- A pinch of salt and black pepper
- ½ tablespoon olive oil
- ½ cup orange juice
- ½ teaspoon orange rind, grated

Directions:
1. In your Crock Pot, mix the carrots with the oil and the other ingredients, toss, put the lid on and cook on Low for 6 hours.
2. Divide between plates and serve as a side dish.

Nutrition Info:
- calories 140, fat 2, fiber 2, carbs 7, protein 6

Dill Cauliflower Mash

Servings: 6 | Cooking Time: 5 Hours

Ingredients:
- 1 cauliflower head, florets separated
- 1/3 cup dill, chopped
- 6 garlic cloves
- 2 tablespoons butter, melted
- A pinch of salt and black pepper

Directions:
1. Put cauliflower in your Crock Pot, add dill, garlic and water to cover cauliflower, cover and cook on High for 5 hours.
2. Drain cauliflower and dill, add salt, pepper and butter, mash using a potato masher, whisk well and serve as a side dish.

Nutrition Info:
- calories 187, fat 4, fiber 5, carbs 12, protein 3

Green Beans Mix

Servings: 12 | Cooking Time: 2 Hours

Ingredients:
- 16 ounces green beans
- ½ cup brown sugar
- ½ cup butter, melted
- ¾ teaspoon soy sauce
- Salt and black pepper to the taste

Directions:
1. In your Crock Pot, mix green beans with sugar, but-
ter, soy sauce, salt and pepper, stir, cover and cook on Low for 2 hours.
2. Divide between plates and serve as a side dish.

Nutrition Info:
- calories 176, fat 4, fiber 7, carbs 14, protein 4

Garlic Butter Green Beans

Servings: 6 | Cooking Time: 2 Hours

Ingredients:
- 22 ounces green beans
- 2 garlic cloves, minced
- ¼ cup butter, soft
- 2 tablespoons parmesan, grated

Directions:
1. In your Crock Pot, mix green beans with garlic, butter and parmesan, toss, cover and cook on High for 2 hours.
2. Divide between plates, sprinkle parmesan all over and serve as a side dish.

Nutrition Info:
- calories 60, fat 4, fiber 1, carbs 3, protein 1

Pink Salt Rice

Servings: 8 | Cooking Time: 5 Hours

Ingredients:
- 1 tsp salt
- 2 and ½ cups of water
- 2 cups pink rice

Directions:
1. Add rice, salt, and water to the Crock Pot.
2. Put the cooker's lid on and set the cooking time to 5 hours on Low settings.
3. Serve warm.

Nutrition Info:
- Per Serving: Calories: 120, Total Fat: 3g, Fiber: 3g, Total Carbs: 16g, Protein: 4g

Chapter 10 Snack Recipes

Chapter 10 Snack Recipes

Apple Dip

Servings: 8 | Cooking Time: 1 Hour And 30 Minutes

Ingredients:
- 5 apples, peeled and chopped
- ½ teaspoon cinnamon powder
- 12 ounces jarred caramel sauce
- A pinch of nutmeg, ground

Directions:
1. In your Crock Pot, mix apples with cinnamon, caramel sauce and nutmeg, stir, cover and cook on High for 1 hour and 30 minutes.
2. Divide into bowls and serve.

Nutrition Info:
- calories 200, fat 3, fiber 6, carbs 10, protein 5

Apple Sausage Snack

Servings: 15 | Cooking Time: 2 Hrs

Ingredients:
- 2 lbs. sausages, sliced
- 18 oz. apple jelly
- 9 oz. Dijon mustard

Directions:
1. Add sausage slices, apple jelly, and mustard to the Crock Pot.
2. Put the cooker's lid on and set the cooking time to 2 hours on Low settings.
3. Serve fresh.

Nutrition Info:
- Per Serving: Calories: 200, Total Fat: 3g, Fiber: 1g, Total Carbs: 9g, Protein: 10g

Spinach Dip

Servings: 2 | Cooking Time: 1 Hour

Ingredients:
- 2 tablespoons heavy cream
- ½ cup Greek yogurt
- ½ pound baby spinach
- 2 garlic cloves, minced
- Salt and black pepper to the taste

Directions:
1. In your Crock Pot, mix the spinach with the cream and the other ingredients, toss, put the lid on and cook on High for 1 hour.
2. Blend using an immersion blender, divide into bowls and serve as a party dip.

Nutrition Info:
- calories 221, fat 5, fiber 7, carbs 12, protein 5

Spicy Dip

Servings: 10 | Cooking Time: 3 Hours

Ingredients:
- 1 pound spicy sausage, chopped
- 8 ounces cream cheese, soft
- 8 ounces sour cream
- 20 ounces canned tomatoes and green chilies, chopped

Directions:
1. In your Crock Pot, mix sausage with cream cheese, sour cream and tomatoes and chilies, stir, cover and cook on Low for 3 hours.
2. Divide into bowls and serve as a snack.

Nutrition Info:
- calories 300, fat 12, fiber 7, carbs 30, protein 34

Corn Dip

Servings: 2 | Cooking Time: 2 Hours

Ingredients:
- 1 cup corn
- 1 tablespoon chives, chopped
- ½ cup heavy cream
- 2 ounces cream cheese, cubed
- ¼ teaspoon chili powder

Directions:
1. In your Crock Pot, mix the corn with the chives and the other ingredients, whisk, put the lid on and cook on Low for 2 hours.
2. Divide into bowls and serve as a dip.

Nutrition Info:
- calories 272, fat 5, fiber 10, carbs 12, protein 4

Apple Jelly Sausage Snack

Servings: 15 | Cooking Time: 2 Hours

Ingredients:
- 2 pounds sausages, sliced
- 18 ounces apple jelly
- 9 ounces Dijon mustard

Directions:
1. Place sausage slices in your Crock Pot, add apple jelly and mustard, toss to coat well, cover and cook on Low for 2 hours.
2. Divide into bowls and serve as a snack.

Nutrition Info:
- calories 200, fat 3, fiber 1, carbs 9, protein 10

Roasted Parmesan Green Beans

Servings: 8 (4.4 Ounces Per Serving)
Cooking Time: 4 Hours And 5 Minutes

Ingredients:
- 2 lbs. green beans, fresh, trimmed
- 2 tablespoons olive oil
- 1 teaspoon salt and black pepper
- ½ cup Parmesan cheese, grated

Directions:
1. Rinse and pat dry green beans with paper towel. Drizzle with olive oil and sprinkle with salt and pepper. Using your fingers coat the beans evenly with olive oil and spread them out do not overlap them. Place green beans in greased Crock-Pot. Sprinkle with Parmesan cheese. Cover and cook on HIGH for 3-4 hours. Serve.

Nutrition Info:
- Calories: 91.93, Total Fat: 5.41 g, Saturated Fat: 1.6 g, Cholesterol: 5.5 mg, Sodium: 337.43 mg, Potassium: 247.12 mg, Total Carbohydrates: 6.16 g, Fiber: 3.06 g, Sugar: 3.75 g, Protein: 4.48 g

Lemony Artichokes

Servings: 4 (5.2 Ounces Per Serving)
Cooking Time: 4 Hours And 10 Minutes

Ingredients:
- 4 artichokes
- 2 tablespoons coconut butter, melted
- 3 tablespoons lemon juice
- 1 teaspoon sea salt
- Ground black pepper to taste

Directions:
1. Wash the artichokes. Pull off the outermost leaves until you get to the lighter yellow leaves. Cut off the top third or so of the artichokes. Trim the bottom of the stems. Place in Crock-Pot. Mix together lemon juice, salt, and melted coconut butter and pour over artichokes. Cover and cook on LOW for 6-8 hours or on HIGH for 3-4 hours. Serve.

Nutrition Info:
- Calories: 113.58, Total Fat: 5.98 g, Saturated Fat: 3.7 g, Cholesterol: 15.27 mg, Sodium: 702.59 mg, Potassium: 487.2 mg, Total Carbohydrates: 8.25 g, Fiber: 6.95 g, Sugar: 1.56 g, Protein: 4.29 g

Onion Dip

Servings: 6 | Cooking Time: 1 Hour

Ingredients:
- 8 ounces cream cheese, soft
- ¾ cup sour cream
- 1 cup cheddar cheese, shredded
- 10 bacon slices, cooked and chopped
- 2 yellow onions, chopped

Directions:
1. In your Crock Pot, mix cream cheese with sour cream, cheddar cheese, bacon and onion, stir, cover and cook on High for 1 hour.
2. Divide into bowls and serve.

Nutrition Info:
- calories 222, fat 4, fiber 6, carbs 17, protein 4

Salsa Beans Dip

Servings: 2 | Cooking Time: 1 Hour

Ingredients:
- ¼ cup salsa
- 1 cup canned red kidney beans, drained and rinsed
- ½ cup mozzarella, shredded
- 1 tablespoon green onions, chopped

Directions:
1. In your Crock Pot, mix the salsa with the beans and the other ingredients, toss, put the lid on cook on High for 1 hour.
2. Divide into bowls and serve as a party dip

Nutrition Info:
- calories 302, fat 5, fiber 10, carbs 16, protein 6

Almond Buns

Servings: 6 (1.9 Ounces Per Serving)
Cooking Time: 20 Minutes

Ingredients:
- 3 cups almond flour
- 5 tablespoons butter
- 1 ½ teaspoons sweetener of your choice (optional)
- 2 eggs
- 1 ½ teaspoons baking powder

Directions:
1. In a mixing bowl, combine the dry ingredients. In another bowl, whisk the eggs. Add melted butter to mixture and mix well. Divide almond mixture equally into 6 parts. Grease the bottom of Crock-Pot and place in 6 almond buns. Cover and cook on HIGH for 2 to 2 ½ hours or LOW for 4 to 4 ½ hours. Serve hot.

Nutrition Info:
- Calories: 219.35, Total Fat: 20.7 g, Saturated Fat: 7.32 g, Cholesterol: 87.44 mg, Sodium: 150.31 mg, Potassium: 145.55 mg, Total Carbohydrates: 4.59 g, Fiber: 1.8 g, Sugar: 1.6 g, Protein: 6.09 g

Bourbon Sausage Bites

Servings: 12 | Cooking Time: 3 Hours And 5 Minutes

Ingredients:
- 1/3 cup bourbon
- 1 pound smoked sausage, sliced
- 12 ounces chili sauce
- ¼ cup brown sugar
- 2 tablespoons yellow onion, grated

Directions:
1. Heat up a pan over medium-high heat, add sausage slices, brown them for 2 minutes on each side, drain them on paper towels and transfer to your Crock Pot.
2. Add chili sauce, sugar, onion and bourbon, toss to coat, cover and cook on Low for 3 hours.
3. Divide into bowls and serve as a snack.

Nutrition Info:
- calories 190, fat 11, fiber 1, carbs 12, protein 5

Beer And Cheese Dip

Servings: 10 | Cooking Time: 1 Hour

Ingredients:
- 12 ounces cream cheese
- 6 ounces beer
- 4 cups cheddar cheese, shredded
- 1 tablespoon chives, chopped

Directions:
1. In your Crock Pot, mix cream cheese with beer and cheddar, stir, cover and cook on Low for 1 hour.
2. Stir your dip, add chives, divide into bowls and serve.

Nutrition Info:
- calories 212, fat 4, fiber 7, carbs 16, protein 5

Onion Dip

Servings: 2 | Cooking Time: 8 Hours

Ingredients:
- 2 cups yellow onions, chopped
- A pinch of salt and black pepper
- 1 tablespoon olive oil
- ½ cup heavy cream
- 2 tablespoons mayonnaise

Directions:
1. In your Crock Pot, mix the onions with the cream and the other ingredients, whisk, put the lid on and cook on Low for 8 hours.
2. Divide into bowls and serve as a party dip.

Nutrition Info:
- calories 240, fat 4, fiber 4, carbs 9, protein 7

Crispy Sweet Potatoes With Paprika

Servings: 4 (3.2 Ounces Per Serving)
Cooking Time: 4 Hours And 45 Minutes

Ingredients:
- 2 medium sweet potatoes
- 2 tablespoons olive oil
- 1 teaspoon Cayenne pepper, optional
- 1 tablespoon nutritional yeast, optional
- Sea salt

Directions:
1. Wash and peel the sweet potatoes. Slice them into wedges. In a bowl, mix the potatoes with the other ingredients. Grease the bottom of Crock-Pot and

place the sweet potato wedges in it. Cover and cook on LOW for 4- 4 ½ hours. Serve hot.

Nutrition Info:
- Calories: 120.72, Total Fat: 7.02 g, Saturated Fat: 0.98 g, Cholesterol: 0 mg, Sodium: 37.07 mg, Potassium: 260.14 mg, Total Carbohydrates: 9.06 g, Fiber: 2.57 g, Sugar: 2.9 g

Spinach And Walnuts Dip

Servings: 2 | Cooking Time: 2 Hours

Ingredients:
- ½ cup heavy cream
- ½ cup walnuts, chopped
- 1 cup baby spinach
- 1 garlic clove, chopped
- 1 tablespoon mayonnaise
- Salt and black pepper to the taste

Directions:
1. In your Crock Pot, mix the spinach with the walnuts and the other ingredients, toss, put the lid on and cook on High for 2 hours.
2. Blend using an immersion blender, divide into bowls and serve as a party dip.

Nutrition Info:
- calories 260, fat 4, fiber 2, carbs 12, protein 5

Sauerkraut Dip

Servings: 12 | Cooking Time: 2 Hours

Ingredients:
- 15 ounces canned sauerkraut, drained
- 8 ounces sour cream
- 4 ounces cream cheese
- 4 ounces corned beef, chopped
- 8 ounces Swiss cheese, shredded

Directions:
1. In your Crock Pot, mix sauerkraut with sour cream, cream cheese, beef and Swiss cheese, stir, cover and cook on Low for 2 hours.
2. Divide into bowls and serve.

Nutrition Info:
- calories 166, fat 14, fiber 1, carbs 4, protein 7

Caramel Dip

Servings: 4 | Cooking Time: 2 Hours

Ingredients:
- 1 cup butter
- 12 ounces condensed milk
- 2 cups brown sugar
- 1 cup corn syrup

Directions:
1. In your Crock Pot, mix butter with condensed milk, sugar and corn syrup, cover and cook on High for 2 hours stirring often.
2. Divide into bowls and serve.

Nutrition Info:
- calories 172, fat 2, fiber 6, carbs 12, protein 4

Bean Dip

Servings: 56 | Cooking Time: 3 Hours

Ingredients:
- 16 ounces Mexican cheese
- 5 ounces canned green chilies
- 16 ounces canned refried beans
- 2 pounds tortilla chips
- Cooking spray

Directions:
1. Grease your Crock Pot with cooking spray, line it, add Mexican cheese, green chilies and refried beans, stir, cover and cook on Low for 3 hours.
2. Divide into bowls and serve with tortilla chips on the side.

Nutrition Info:
- calories 120, fat 2, fiber 1, carbs 14, protein 3

Slow-cooked Lemon Peel

Servings: 80 Pieces

Cooking Time: 4 Hrs

Ingredients:
- 5 big lemons, peel cut into strips
- 2 and ¼ cups white sugar
- 5 cups of water

Directions:
1. Spread the lemon peel in the Crock Pot and top it with sugar and water.
2. Put the cooker's lid on and set the cooking time to 4 hours on Low settings.

3. Drain the cooked peel and serve.

Nutrition Info:
- Per Serving: Calories: 7, Total Fat: 1g, Fiber: 1g, Total Carbs: 2g, Protein: 1g

Caramel Milk Dip

Servings: 4 | Cooking Time: 2 Hours

Ingredients:
- 1 cup butter
- 12 oz. condensed milk
- 2 cups brown sugar
- 1 cup of corn syrup

Directions:
1. Add butter, milk, corn syrup, and sugar to the Crock Pot.
2. Put the cooker's lid on and set the cooking time to 2 hours on High settings.
3. Serve warm.

Nutrition Info:
- Per Serving: Calories: 172, Total Fat: 2g, Fiber: 6g, Total Carbs: 12g, Protein: 4g

Peanut Snack

Servings: 4 | Cooking Time: 1 Hour And 30 Minutes

Ingredients:
- 1 cup peanuts
- 1 cup chocolate peanut butter
- 12 ounces dark chocolate chips
- 12 ounces white chocolate chips

Directions:
1. In your Crock Pot, mix peanuts with peanut butter, dark and white chocolate chips, cover and cook on Low for 1 hour and 30 minutes.
2. Divide this mix into small muffin cups, leave aside to cool down and serve as a snack.

Nutrition Info:
- calories 200, fat 4, fiber 6, carbs 10, protein 5

Cheese Onion Dip

Servings: 6 | Cooking Time: 1 Hour

Ingredients:
- 8 oz. cream cheese, soft
- ¾ cup sour cream
- 1 cup cheddar cheese, shredded

- 10 bacon slices, cooked and chopped
- 2 yellow onions, chopped

Directions:
1. Add cream cheese, bacon and all other ingredients to the Crock Pot.
2. Put the cooker's lid on and set the cooking time to 1 hour on High settings.
3. Serve.

Nutrition Info:
- Per Serving: Calories: 222, Total Fat: 4g, Fiber: 6g, Total Carbs: 17g, Protein: 4g

Cinnamon Pecans Snack

Servings: 2 | Cooking Time: 3 Hours

Ingredients:
- ½ tablespoon cinnamon powder
- ¼ cup water
- ½ tablespoon avocado oil
- ½ teaspoon chili powder
- 2 cups pecans

Directions:
1. In your Crock Pot, mix the pecans with the cinnamon and the other ingredients, toss, put the lid on and cook on Low for 3 hours.
2. Divide the pecans into bowls and serve as a snack.

Nutrition Info:
- calories 172, fat 3, fiber 5, carbs 8, protein 2

Salmon Bites

Servings: 2 | Cooking Time: 2 Hours

Ingredients:
- 1 pound salmon fillets, boneless
- ¼ cup chili sauce
- A pinch of salt and black pepper
- ½ teaspoon turmeric powder
- 2 tablespoons grape jelly

Directions:
1. In your Crock Pot, mix the salmon with the chili sauce and the other ingredients, toss gently, put the lid on and cook on High for 2 hours.
2. Serve as an appetizer.

Nutrition Info:
- calories 200, fat 6, fiber 3, carbs 15, protein 12

Almond Spread

Servings: 2 | Cooking Time: 8 Hours

Ingredients:
- ¼ cup almonds
- 1 cup heavy cream
- ½ teaspoon nutritional yeast flakes
- A pinch of salt and black pepper

Directions:

1. In your Crock Pot, mix the almonds with the cream and the other ingredients, toss, put the lid on and cook on Low for 8 hours.
2. Transfer to a blender, pulse well, divide into bowls and serve.

Nutrition Info:
- calories 270, fat 4, fiber 4, carbs 8, protein 10

Almond Bowls

Servings: 2 | Cooking Time: 4 Hours

Ingredients:
- 1 tablespoon cinnamon powder
- 1 cup sugar
- 2 cups almonds
- ½ cup water
- ½ teaspoons vanilla extract

Directions:

1. In your Crock Pot, mix the almonds with the cinnamon and the other ingredients, toss, put the lid on and cook on Low for 4 hours.
2. Divide into bowls and serve as a snack.

Nutrition Info:
- calories 260, fat 3, fiber 4, carbs 12, protein 8

Beans Spread

Servings: 2 | Cooking Time: 6 Hours

Ingredients:
- 1 cup canned black beans, drained
- 2 tablespoons tahini paste
- ½ teaspoon balsamic vinegar
- ¼ cup veggie stock
- ½ tablespoon olive oil

Directions:

1. In your Crock Pot, mix the beans with the tahini paste and the other ingredients, toss, put the lid on and cook on Low for 6 hours.

2. Transfer to your food processor, blend well, divide into bowls and serve.

Nutrition Info:
- calories 221, fat 6, fiber 5, carbs 19, protein 3

White Bean Spread

Servings: 4 | Cooking Time: 7 Hours

Ingredients:
- ½ cup white beans, dried
- 2 tablespoons cashews, chopped
- 1 teaspoon apple cider vinegar
- 1 cup veggie stock
- 1 tablespoon water

Directions:

1. In your Crock Pot, mix beans with cashews and stock, stir, cover and cook on Low for 6 hours.
2. Drain, transfer to your food processor, add vinegar and water, pulse well, divide into bowls and serve as a spread.

Nutrition Info:
- calories 221, fat 6, fiber 5, carbs 19, protein 3

Spaghetti Squash

Servings: 6 (6.8 Ounces)

Cooking Time: 6 Hours

Ingredients:
- 1 spaghetti squash (vegetable spaghetti)
- 4 tablespoon olive oil
- 1 ¾ cups water
- Sea salt

Directions:

1. Slice the squash in half lengthwise and scoop out the seeds. Drizzle the halves with olive oil and season with sea salt. Place the squash in Crock-Pot and add the water. Close the lid and cook on LOW for 4-6 hours. Remove the squash and allow it to cool for about 30 minutes. Use a fork to scrape out spaghetti squash.

Nutrition Info:
- Calories: 130.59, Total Fat: 9.11 g, Saturated Fat: 1.27 g, Cholesterol: 0 mg, Sodium: 6.79 mg, Potassium: 399.95 mg, Total Carbohydrates: 13.26 g, Fiber: 2.27 g, Sugar: 2.49 g, Protein: 1.13 g

Chapter 11 Dessert Recipes

Chapter 11 Dessert Recipes

Nutty Caramel Apples

Servings: 6 | Cooking Time: 4 Hrs.

Ingredients:
- 6 gala apples, cut in half and deseeded
- 8 oz caramel, package
- 5 tbsp water
- 3 tbsp walnuts, crushed

Directions:
1. Toss the apples with water, caramel, and walnuts in an insert of Crock Pot.
2. Put the cooker's lid on and set the cooking time to 3 hours on Low settings.
3. Serve when chilled.

Nutrition Info:
- Per Serving: Calories: 307, Total Fat: 12g, Fiber: 5g, Total Carbs: 47.17g, Protein: 4g

Chocolate And Liquor Cream

Servings: 4 | Cooking Time: 2 Hours

Ingredients:
- 3.5 ounces crème fraiche
- 3.5 ounces dark chocolate, cut into chunks
- 1 teaspoon liquor
- 1 teaspoon sugar

Directions:
1. In your Crock Pot, mix crème fraiche with chocolate, liquor and sugar, stir, cover, cook on Low for 2 hours, divide into bowls and serve cold

Nutrition Info:
- calories 200, fat 12, fiber 4, carbs 6, protein 3

Espresso Mousse Drink

Servings:1 | Cooking Time: 1 Hour

Ingredients:
- ½ cup milk
- 1 teaspoon instant coffee
- ¼ cup of water

Directions:
1. Mix instant coffee with water.
2. Then pour milk in the Crock Pot and cook it on High for 1 hour.
3. Meanwhile, blend the coffee mixture with the help of the hand blender until you get fluffy foam.
4. Transfer the blended mixture into the glass.
5. Add hot milk.

Nutrition Info:
- Per Serving: 61 calories, 4g protein, 6g carbohydrates, 2.5g fat, 0g fiber, 10mg cholesterol, 59mg sodium, 73mg potassium.

Cinnamon Peach Mix

Servings: 2 | Cooking Time: 2 Hours

Ingredients:
- 2 cups peaches, peeled and halved
- 3 tablespoons sugar
- ½ teaspoon cinnamon powder
- ½ cup heavy cream
- 1 teaspoon vanilla extract

Directions:
1. In your Crock Pot, mix the peaches with the sugar and the other ingredients, toss, put the lid on and cook on High for 2 hours.
2. Divide the mix into bowls and serve.

Nutrition Info:
- calories 212, fat 4, fiber 4, carbs 7, protein 3

Apple Granola Crumble

Servings: 4 | Cooking Time: 6 1/4 Hours

Ingredients:
- 4 red apples, peeled, cored and sliced
- 2 tablespoons honey
- 1 1/2 cups granola
- 1/2 teaspoon cinnamon powder

Directions:
1. Mix the apples and honey in your crock pot.
2. Top with the granola and sprinkle with cinnamon.
3. Cover the pot and cook on low settings for 6 hours.
4. Serve the crumble warm.

Mandarin Cream

Servings: 2 | Cooking Time: 2 Hours

Ingredients:
- 1 tablespoon ginger, grated
- 3 tablespoons sugar
- 3 mandarins, peeled and chopped
- 2 tablespoons agave nectar
- ½ cup coconut cream

Directions:
1. In your Crock Pot, mix the ginger with the sugar, mandarins and the other ingredients, whisk, put the lid on and cook on High for 2 hours.
2. Blend the cream using an immersion blender, divide into bowls and serve cold.

Nutrition Info:
- calories 100, fat 4, fiber 5, carbs 6, protein 7

Sweet Baked Milk

Servings:5 | Cooking Time: 10 Hours

Ingredients:
- 4 cups of milk
- 3 tablespoons sugar
- ½ teaspoon vanilla extract

Directions:
1. Mix milk with sugar and vanilla extract and stir until sugar is dissolved.
2. Then pour the liquid in the Crock Pot and close the lid.
3. Cook the milk on Low for 10 hours.

Nutrition Info:
- Per Serving: 126 calories, 6.4g protein, 16.9g carbohydrates, 4g fat, 3g fiber, 16mg cholesterol, 92mg sodium, 113mg potassium.

Berry Cream

Servings: 2 | Cooking Time: 2 Hours

Ingredients:
- 2 tablespoons cashews, chopped
- 1 cup heavy cream
- ½ cup blueberries
- ½ cup maple syrup
- ½ tablespoon coconut oil, melted

Directions:
1. In your Crock Pot, mix the cream with the berries

and the other ingredients, whisk, put the lid on and cook on Low for 2 hours.
2. Divide the mix into bowls and serve cold.

Nutrition Info:
- calories 200, fat 3, fiber 5, carbs 12, protein 3

Caramel Apple Tart

Servings:4 | Cooking Time: 3.5 Hours

Ingredients:
- 2 tablespoons salted caramel
- 2 apples, sliced
- 1 teaspoon butter
- 5 oz puff pastry
- 1 teaspoon olive oil

Directions:
1. Sprinkle the Crock Pot bowl with olive oil from inside.
2. Then put the puff pastry inside and flatten it in the shape of the pie crust.
3. Grease the pie crust with butter and top with sliced apples.
4. Then sprinkle the apples with salted caramel and close the lid.
5. Cook the apple tart on High for 3.5 hours.

Nutrition Info:
- Per Serving: 291 calories, 3.1g protein, 35.3g carbohydrates, 16.2g fat, 3.2g fiber, 3mg cholesterol, 108mg sodium, 152mg potassium.

Vegan Mousse

Servings:3 | Cooking Time: 2 Hours

Ingredients:
- 1 cup of coconut milk
- 2 tablespoons corn starch
- 1 teaspoon vanilla extract
- 1 avocado, pitted, pilled

Directions:
1. Mix coconut milk and corn starch until smooth and pour in the Crock Pot.
2. Add vanilla extract and cook it on High for 2 hours.
3. Then cool the mixture till room temperature and mix with avocado.
4. Blend the mousse until fluffy and smooth.

Nutrition Info:

- Per Serving: 348 calories, 3.1g protein, 16.4g carbohydrates, 32.1g fat, 6.3g fiber, 0mg cholesterol, 16mg sodium, 537mg potassium.

Quinoa Pudding

Servings: 2 | Cooking Time: 2 Hours

Ingredients:
- 1 cup quinoa
- 2 cups almond milk
- ½ cup sugar
- ½ tablespoon walnuts, chopped
- ½ tablespoon almonds, chopped

Directions:

1. In your Crock Pot, mix the quinoa with the milk and the other ingredients, toss, put the lid on and cook on High for 2 hours.
2. Divide the pudding into cups and serve.

Nutrition Info:
- calories 213, fat 4, fiber 6, carbs 10, protein 4

Easy Monkey Rolls

Servings:8 | Cooking Time: 3 Hours

Ingredients:
- 1 tablespoon liquid honey
- 1 tablespoon sugar
- 2 eggs, beaten
- 1-pound cinnamon rolls, dough
- 2 tablespoons butter, melted

Directions:

1. Cut the cinnamon roll dough on 8 servings.
2. Then line the bottom of the Crock Pot with baking paper and put the rolls inside.
3. In the bowl mix sugar, egg, liquid honey, and butter. Whisk the mixture.
4. Pour the egg mixture over the cinnamon roll dough and flatten well.
5. Close the lid and cook the meal on High for 3 hours.

Nutrition Info:
- Per Serving: 266 calories, 4.9g protein, 32.6g carbohydrates, 13.3g fat, 1.4g fiber, 86mg cholesterol, 253mg sodium, 80mg potassium.

Tapioca Pearls Pudding

Servings: 6 | Cooking Time: 1 Hr.

Ingredients:
- 1 and ¼ cups of milk
- 1/3 cup tapioca pearls, rinsed
- ½ cup of water
- ½ cup of sugar
- Zest of ½ lemon

Directions:

1. Whisk tapioca with milk, sugar, lemon zest, and water in the insert of Crock Pot.
2. Put the cooker's lid on and set the cooking time to 1 hour on Low settings.
3. Serve.

Nutrition Info:
- Per Serving: Calories: 200, Total Fat: 4g, Fiber: 2g, Total Carbs: 37g, Protein: 3g

Pear Apple Jam

Servings: 12 | Cooking Time: 3 Hrs.

Ingredients:
- 8 pears, cored and cut into quarters
- 2 apples, peeled, cored and quartered
- ½ cup apple juice
- 1 tsp cinnamon, ground

Directions:

1. Toss pears, apples, apple juice, and cinnamon in the insert of Crock Pot.
2. Put the cooker's lid on and set the cooking time to 3 hours on High settings.
3. Blend this cooked pears-apples mixture to make a jam.
4. Allow it to cool them divide in the jars.
5. Serve.

Nutrition Info:
- Per Serving: Calories: 100, Total Fat: 1g, Fiber: 2g, Total Carbs: 20g, Protein: 3g

Green Tea Avocado Pudding

Servings: 2 | Cooking Time: 1 Hr.

Ingredients:
- ½ cup of coconut milk
- 1 and ½cup avocado, pitted and peeled
- 2 tbsp green tea powder
- 2 tsp lime zest, grated
- 1 tbsp sugar

Directions:
1. Mix coconut milk with tea powder and rest of the ingredients in the insert of Crock Pot.
2. Put the cooker's lid on and set the cooking time to 1 hour on Low settings.
3. Divide the pudding into the serving cups and allow it to cool.
4. Serve.

Nutrition Info:
- Per Serving: Calories: 107, Total Fat: 5g, Fiber: 3g, Total Carbs: 6g, Protein: 8g

Sugar Almonds

Servings:2 | Cooking Time: 30 Minutes

Ingredients:
- ½ cup almonds
- ½ cup of sugar
- 1 tablespoon butter

Directions:
1. Put butter in the Crock Pot.
2. Add almonds and close the lid.
3. Cook the almond on High for 20 minutes.
4. Then open the lid, mix the almonds, and add sugar.
5. Carefully mix the dessert and cook it for 10 minutes on high.

Nutrition Info:
- Per Serving: 376 calories, 5.1g protein, 55.1g carbohydrates, 17.6g fat, 3g fiber, 15mg cholesterol, 41mg sodium, 176mg potassium.

Stuffed Peaches

Servings:4 | Cooking Time: 20 Minutes

Ingredients:
- 4 peaches, halved, pitted
- 4 pecans
- 1 tablespoon maple syrup
- 2 oz goat cheese, crumbled

Directions:
1. Fill every peach half with pecan and sprinkle with maple syrup.
2. Then put the fruits in the Crock Pot in one layer and top with goat cheese.
3. Close the lid and cook the peaches for 20 minutes on High.

Nutrition Info:
- Per Serving: 234 calories, 7.2g protein, 19.7g carbohydrates, 15.5g fat, 3.8g fiber, 15mg cholesterol, 49mg sodium, 360mg potassium.

Rhubarb Jam

Servings:6 | Cooking Time: 8 Hours

Ingredients:
- 2-pounds rhubarb, chopped
- 1 cup of sugar
- 1 teaspoon lime zest, grated
- ¼ cup of water

Directions:
1. Put all ingredients in the Crock Pot.
2. Cook the jam on Low for 8 hours.
3. Then transfer it in the glass jars and cool well.

Nutrition Info:
- Per Serving: 157 calories, 1.4g protein, 40.2g carbohydrates, 0.3g fat, 2.8g fiber, 0mg cholesterol, 6mg sodium, 436mg potassium.

Vanilla Pears

Servings: 2 | Cooking Time: 2 Hours

Ingredients:
- 2 tablespoons avocado oil
- 1 teaspoon vanilla extract
- 2 pears, cored and halved
- ½ tablespoon lime juice
- 1 tablespoon sugar

Directions:
1. In your Crock Pot combine the pears with the sugar, oil and the other ingredients, toss, put the lid on and cook on High for 2 hours.
2. Divide between plates and serve.

Nutrition Info:
- calories 200, fat 4, fiber 6, carbs 16, protein 3

Tarragon Peach Confiture

Servings:6 | Cooking Time: 2.5 Hours

Ingredients:
- 1-pound peaches, pitted, halved
- ½ cup of sugar
- 1 teaspoon lemon zest, grated
- 1 teaspoon dried tarragon
- 1/3 cup water

Directions:

1. Put all ingredients in the Crock Pot and close the lid.
2. Cook the dessert on high for 5 hours.
3. Cool the cooked confiture well.

Nutrition Info:
- Per Serving: 73 calories, 0.3g protein, 19.1g carbohydrates, 0.1g fat, 0.4g fiber, 0mg cholesterol, 0mg sodium, 52mg potassium.

Lemony Orange Marmalade

Servings: 8 | Cooking Time: 3 Hrs.

Ingredients:
- Juice of 2 lemons
- 3 lbs. sugar
- 1 lb. oranges, peeled and cut into segments
- 1-pint water

Directions:

1. Whisk lemon juice, sugar, water, and oranges in the insert of Crock Pot.
2. Put the cooker's lid on and set the cooking time to 3 hours on High settings.
3. Serve when chilled.

Nutrition Info:
- Per Serving: Calories: 100, Total Fat: 4g, Fiber: 4g, Total Carbs: 12g, Protein: 4g

Jelly Bears

Servings:4 | Cooking Time: 1 Hour

Ingredients:
- 1 cup of orange juice
- ¼ cup of water
- 3 tablespoons gelatin

Directions:

1. Pour orange juice in the Crock Pot and cook it on High for 1 hour.

2. Meanwhile, mix water with gelatin and leave for 10-15 minutes.
3. When the orange juice is cooked, cool it for 10-15 minutes and add gelatin mixture.
4. Mix the liquid until smooth.
5. Then pour it in the jelly molds (in the shape of bears) and refrigerate for as minimum 40 minutes.

Nutrition Info:
- Per Serving: 46 calories, 4.9g protein, 6.5g carbohydrates, 0.1g fat, 0.1g fiber, 0mg cholesterol, 11mg sodium, 125mg potassium.

Apricot And Peaches Cream

Servings: 2 | Cooking Time: 2 Hours

Ingredients:
- 1 cup apricots, pitted and chopped
- 1 cup peaches, pitted and chopped
- 1 cup heavy cream
- 3 tablespoons brown sugar
- 1 teaspoon vanilla extract

Directions:

1. In a blender, mix the apricots with the peaches and the other ingredients, and pulse well.
2. Put the cream in the Crock Pot, put the lid on, cook on High for 2 hours, divide into bowls and serve.

Nutrition Info:
- calories 200, fat 4, fiber 5, carbs 10, protein 4

Melon Pudding

Servings:3 | Cooking Time: 3 Hours

Ingredients:
- 1 cup melon, chopped
- ¼ cup of coconut milk
- 2 tablespoons cornstarch
- 1 teaspoon vanilla extract

Directions:

1. Blend the melon until smooth and mix with coconut milk, cornstarch, and vanilla extract.
2. Transfer the mixture in the Crock Pot and cook the pudding on low for 3 hours.

Nutrition Info:
- Per Serving: 88 calories, 0.9g protein, 10.4g carbohydrates, 4.9g fat, 1g fiber, 0mg cholesterol, 12mg sodium, 194mg potassium.

Peanut Sweets

Servings:8 | Cooking Time: 4 Hours

Ingredients:
- 1 cup peanuts, roasted, chopped
- 1 cup of chocolate chips
- ¼ cup heavy cream

Directions:
1. Put chocolate chips and heavy cream in the Crock Pot.
2. Cook the mixture on low for 4 hours.
3. Then mix the mixture until smooth and add roasted peanuts.
4. Carefully mix the mixture again.
5. Line the baking tray with baking paper.
6. With the help of the spoon, make the medium size balls (sweets) and put on the baking paper.
7. Cool the sweets until they are solid.

Nutrition Info:
- Per Serving: 229 calories, 6.4g protein, 15.5g carbohydrates, 16.6g fat, 2.3g fiber, 10mg cholesterol, 21mg sodium, 210mg potassium.

Clove Pastry Wheels

Servings:4 | Cooking Time: 3 Hours

Ingredients:
- 1 teaspoon ground clove
- 4 oz puff pastry
- 1 tablespoon brown sugar
- 1 tablespoon butter, softened

Directions:
1. Roll up the puff pastry into a square.
2. Then grease the puff pastry with butter and sprinkle with ground clove.
3. Roll it in the shape of a log and cut it into pieces (wheels).
4. Put the baking paper at the bottom of the Crock Pot.
5. Then put puff pastry wheels inside in one layer and close the lid.
6. Cook the meal on High for 3 hours.

Nutrition Info:
- Per Serving: 192 calories, 2.1g protein, 15.3g carbohydrates, 13.8g fat, 0.6g fiber, 8mg cholesterol, 93mg sodium, 27mg potassium.

Apple Dump Cake

Servings: 8 | Cooking Time: 4 1/2 Hours

Ingredients:
- 6 Granny Smith apples, peeled, cored and sliced
- 1/4 cup light brown sugar
- 1 teaspoon cinnamon
- 1 box yellow cake mix
- 1/2 cup butter, melted

Directions:
1. Mix the apples, brown sugar and cinnamon in a Crock Pot.
2. Top with the cake mix and drizzle with butter.
3. Cover the pot and cook on low settings for 4 hours.
4. Allow the cake to cool in the pot before serving.

Choco Liquor Crème

Servings: 4 | Cooking Time: 2 Hrs.

Ingredients:
- 3.5 oz. crème Fraiche
- 3.5 oz. dark chocolate, cut into chunks
- 1 tsp liquor
- 1 tsp sugar

Directions:
1. Whisk crème Fraiche with sugar, liquor, and chocolate in the insert of Crock Pot.
2. Put the cooker's lid on and set the cooking time to 2 hours on High settings.
3. Serve chilled.

Nutrition Info:
- Per Serving: Calories: 200, Total Fat: 12g, Fiber: 4g, Total Carbs: 6g, Protein: 3g

Cocoa Peanut Candies

Servings: 11 | Cooking Time: 2.5 Hrs.

Ingredients:
- 6 tbsp, peanuts, roasted and crushed
- 8 oz dark chocolate, crushed
- ¼ cup of cocoa powder
- 4 tbsp chocolate chips
- 3 tbsp heavy cream

Directions:
1. Add roasted peanuts and rest of the ingredients to the insert of Crock Pot.
2. Put the cooker's lid on and set the cooking time to

5 hours on Low settings.

3. Divide this chocolate mixture into a silicone candy molds tray.

4. Place this tray in the refrigerator for 2 hours.

5. Serve.

Nutrition Info:
- Per Serving: Calories: 229, Total Fat: 15.8g, Fiber: 3g, Total Carbs: 19.02g, Protein: 5g

White Wine Chocolate

Servings:2 | Cooking Time: 3 Hours

Ingredients:
- 1 tablespoon cocoa powder
- 2 teaspoons sugar
- 3 cups white wine
- ¼ cup of chocolate chips
- 1 teaspoon vanilla extract

Directions:
1. Put all ingredients in the Crock Pot.
2. Close the lid.
3. Cook the dessert on Low for 3 hours.
4. Then carefully mix it and pour it in the glasses.

Nutrition Info:
- Per Serving: 289 calories, 1.6g protein, 18.6g carbohydrates, 4.4g fat, 1g fiber, 3mg cholesterol, 23mg sodium, 333mg potassium.

Lemon Apple Slices

Servings:2 | Cooking Time: 3 Hours

Ingredients:
- 2 apples, sliced
- 2 tablespoons lemon juice
- 1 tablespoon maple syrup
- 2 tablespoons butter

Directions:
1. Sprinkle the apples with lemon juice and put them in the Crock Pot.
2. Add butter and maple syrup.
3. Close the lid and cook the apples on low for 3 hours.

Nutrition Info:
- Per Serving: 248 calories, 0.8g protein, 37.8g carbohydrates, 12.1g fat, 5.5g fiber, 31mg cholesterol, 88mg sodium, 281mg potassium.

Vanilla Crème Cups

Servings: 4 | Cooking Time: 3 Hrs.

Ingredients:
- 1 tbsp vanilla extract
- 1 cup of sugar
- ½ cup heavy cream, whipped
- 7 egg yolks, whisked

Directions:
1. Mix egg yolks with sugar, vanilla extract, and cream in a mixer.
2. Pour this creamy mixture into 4 ramekins.
3. Pour 1 cup water into the insert of Crock Pot.
4. Place the ramekins the cooker.
5. Put the cooker's lid on and set the cooking time to 3 hours on Low settings.
6. Serve.

Nutrition Info:
- Per Serving: Calories: 254, Total Fat: 13.5g, Fiber: 0g, Total Carbs: 26.84g, Protein: 5g

Cinnamon Plums

Servings: 2 | Cooking Time: 2 Hours

Ingredients:
- ½ pound plums, pitted and halved
- 2 tablespoons sugar
- 1 teaspoon cinnamon, ground
- ½ cup orange juice

Directions:
1. In your Crock Pot, mix the plums with the cinnamon and the other ingredients, toss, put the lid on and cook on Low for 2 hours.
2. Divide into bowls and serve as a dessert.

Nutrition Info:
- calories 180, fat 2, fiber 1, carbs 8, protein 8

Blueberries Jam

Servings: 2 | Cooking Time: 4 Hours

Ingredients:
- 2 cups blueberries
- ½ cup water
- ¼ pound sugar
- Zest of 1 lime

Directions:
1. In your Crock Pot, combine the berries with the

water and the other ingredients, toss, put the lid on and cook on High for 4 hours.
2. Divide into small jars and serve cold.

Nutrition Info:
- calories 250, fat 3, fiber 2, carbs 6, protein 1

Strawberry Marmalade

Servings:8 | Cooking Time: 4 Hours

Ingredients:
- 2 cups strawberries, chopped
- 1 cup of sugar
- ¼ cup lemon juice
- 2 oz water

Directions:
1. Put all ingredients in the Crock Pot and gently mix.
2. Then close the lid and cook the mixture on low for 4 hours.
3. Transfer the cooked mixture in the silicone molds and leave to cool for up to 8 hours.

Nutrition Info:
- Per Serving: 107 calories, 0.3g protein, 27.9g carbohydrates, 0.2g fat, 0.8g fiber, 0mg cholesterol, 2mg sodium, 65mg potassium.

Mango Cream Dessert

Servings: 4 | Cooking Time: 1 Hr.

Ingredients:
- 1 mango, sliced
- 14 oz. coconut cream

Directions:
1. Add mango and cream to the insert of Crock Pot.
2. Put the cooker's lid on and set the cooking time to 1 hour on High settings.
3. Serve.

Nutrition Info:
- Per Serving: Calories: 150, Total Fat: 12g, Fiber: 2g, Total Carbs: 6g, Protein: 1g

Bananas And Sweet Sauce

Servings: 4 | Cooking Time: 2 Hours

Ingredients:
- Juice of ½ lemon
- 3 tablespoons agave nectar
- 1 tablespoon vegetable oil

- 4 bananas, peeled and sliced
- ½ teaspoon cardamom seeds

Directions:
1. Put the bananas in your Crock Pot, add agave nectar, lemon juice, oil and cardamom, cover, cook on Low for 2 hours, divide bananas between plates, drizzle agave sauce all over and serve.

Nutrition Info:
- calories 120, fat 1, fiber 2, carbs 8, protein 3

Cherry And Rhubarb Mix

Servings: 2 | Cooking Time: 2 Hours

Ingredients:
- 2 cups rhubarb, sliced
- ½ cup cherries, pitted
- 1 tablespoon butter, melted
- ¼ cup coconut cream
- ½ cup sugar

Directions:
1. In your Crock Pot, mix the rhubarb with the cherries and the other ingredients, toss, put the lid on and cook on High for 2 hours.
2. Divide the mix into bowls and serve cold.

Nutrition Info:
- calories 200, fat 2, fiber 3, carbs 6, protein 1

Apples With Raisins

Servings:4 | Cooking Time: 5 Hours

Ingredients:
- 4 big apples
- 4 teaspoons raisins
- 4 teaspoons sugar
- ½ teaspoon ground cinnamon
- ½ cup of water

Directions:
1. Core the apples and fill them with sugar and raisins.
2. Then arrange the apples in the Crock Pot.
3. Sprinkle them with ground cinnamon.
4. Add water and close the lid.
5. Cook the apples on low for 5 hours.

Nutrition Info:
- Per Serving: 141 calories, 0.7g protein, 37.4g carbohydrates, 0.4g fat, 5.7g fiber, 0mg cholesterol, 3mg sodium, 263mg potassium.

Banana Muffins

Servings:2 | Cooking Time: 2.5 Hours

Ingredients:
- 2 eggs, beaten
- 2 bananas, chopped
- 4 tablespoons flour
- ½ teaspoon vanilla extract
- ½ teaspoon baking powder

Directions:
1. Mash the chopped bananas and mix them with eggs.
2. Then add vanilla extract and baking powder.
3. Add flour and stir the mixture until smooth.
4. Pour the banana mixture in the muffin molds (fill ½ part of every muffin mold) and transfer in the Crock Pot.
5. Cook the muffins on High for 2.5 hours.

Nutrition Info:
- Per Serving: 229 calories, 84g protein, 39.9g carbohydrates, 4.9g fat, 3.5g fiber, 164mg cholesterol, 64mg sodium, 626mg potassium.

Apple Cobbler

Servings:2 | Cooking Time: 2 Hours

Ingredients:
- 1 cup apples, diced
- 1 teaspoon ground cinnamon
- ½ cup flour
- 2 tablespoons coconut oil
- ½ cup cream

Directions:
1. Mix flour with sugar and coconut oil and knead the dough.
2. Then mix apples with ground cinnamon and place it in the Crock Pot in one layer.
3. Grate the dough over the apples and add cream.
4. Close the lid and cook the cobbler on High for 2 hours.

Nutrition Info:
- Per Serving: 330 calories, 4.1g protein, 42.1g carbohydrates, 17.5g fat, 4.2g fiber, 11mg cholesterol, 21mg sodium, 180mg potassium.

Cinnamon Plum Jam

Servings:6 | Cooking Time: 6 Hours

Ingredients:
- 4 cups plums, pitted, halved
- 1 tablespoon ground cinnamon
- ½ cup brown sugar
- 1 teaspoon vanilla extract

Directions:
1. Put all ingredients in the Crock Pot and gently mix.
2. Close the lid and cook it on Low for 6 hours.

Nutrition Info:
- Per Serving: 71 calories, 0.4g protein, 18.2g carbohydrates, 0.1g fat, 1.2g fiber, 0mg cholesterol, 4mg sodium, 91mg potassium.

Flax Seeds Bars

Servings:8 | Cooking Time: 4 Hours

Ingredients:
- 1 cup flax seeds
- 1 cup of chocolate chips
- ¼ cup cream
- 3 oz nuts, chopped
- 1 tablespoon coconut oil

Directions:
1. Line the Crock Pot bottom with baking paper.
2. Then put all ingredients inside and close the lid.
3. Cook the mixture on low for 4 hours.
4. Then open the lid and make the mixture homogenous.
5. Transfer it in the silicone mold and flatten well.
6. Refrigerate it until solid and crush into bars.

Nutrition Info:
- Per Serving: 269 calories, 6.1g protein, 19.4g carbohydrates, 18.2g fat, 5.5g fiber, 6mg cholesterol, 94mg sodium, 258mg potassium.

Caramel Pie

Servings:6 | Cooking Time: 2 Hours

Ingredients:
- 1 cup vanilla cake mix
- 4 eggs, beaten
- 1 teaspoon butter, melted
- 4 caramels, candy, crushed

Directions:

1. Mix vanilla cake mix with eggs and butter.
2. Pour the liquid in the Crock Pot and sprinkle with crushed candies.
3. Close the lid and cook the pie on high for 2 hours.
4. Then cool it and remove from the Crock Pot.
5. Cut the pie into 6 servings.

Nutrition Info:
- Per Serving: 173 calories, 4g protein, 30.1g carbohydrates, 4.1g fat, 0.7g fiber, 111mg cholesterol, 355mg sodium, 54mg potassium.

Panna Cotta

Servings:2 | Cooking Time: 1.5 Hours

Ingredients:
- 1 tablespoon gelatin
- 1 cup cream
- ¼ cup of sugar
- 2 tablespoons strawberry jam

Directions:
1. Pour cream in the Crock Pot.
2. Add sugar and close the lid.
3. Cook the liquid on High for 1.5 hours.
4. Then cool it to the room temperature, add gelatin, and mix until smooth.
5. Pour the liquid in the glasses and refrigerate until solid.
6. Top every cream jelly with jam.

Nutrition Info:
- Per Serving: 270 calories, 7g protein, 47.4g carbohydrates, 6.7g fat, 0g fiber, 23mg cholesterol, 53mg sodium, 45mg potassium.

Berry Pudding

Servings:2 | Cooking Time: 5 Hours

Ingredients:
- ¼ cup strawberries, chopped
- 2 tablespoons sugar
- 2 cups of milk
- 1 tablespoon corn starch
- 1 teaspoon vanilla extract

Directions:
1. Mix milk with corn starch and pour liquid in the Crock Pot.
2. Add vanilla extract, sugar, and strawberries.
3. Close the lid and cook the pudding on low for 5

hours.
4. Carefully mix the dessert before serving.

Nutrition Info:
- Per Serving: 196 calories, 8.1g protein, 30.2g carbohydrates, 5.1g fat, 0.4g fiber, 20mg cholesterol, 115mg sodium, 171mg potassium.

Chocolate Pudding

Servings: 4 | Cooking Time: 1 Hour

Ingredients:
- 4 ounces heavy cream
- 4 ounces dark chocolate, cut into chunks
- 1 teaspoon sugar

Directions:
1. In a bowl, mix the cream with chocolate and sugar, whisk well, pour into your Crock Pot, cover and cook on High for 1 hour.
2. Divide into bowls and serve cold.

Nutrition Info:
- calories 232, fat 12, fiber 6, carbs 9, protein 4

Orange Cake

Servings:12 | Cooking Time: 2 Hours

Ingredients:
- 2 cups of orange juice
- ½ cup poppy seeds
- ½ cup olive oil
- 2 cups semolina
- ½ cup of sugar

Directions:
1. Mix orange juice with poppy seeds, olive oil, sugar, and semolina.
2. Then pour the liquid in the Crock Pot.
3. Cook it on High for 2 hours.
4. When the cooking time is finished, let the cake to cool to the room temperature, remove it from the Crock Pot and cut into servings.

Nutrition Info:
- Per Serving: 252 calories, 4.8g protein, 34.2g carbohydrates, 11.3g fat, 1.7g fiber, 0mg cholesterol, 2mg sodium, 174mg potassium.

Banana Ice Cream

Servings:2 | Cooking Time: 5 Hours

Ingredients:
- ½ cup cream
- 4 tablespoons sugar
- 4 bananas, chopped
- 2 egg yolks

Directions:
1. Mix sugar with egg yolks and blend until you get a lemon color mixture.
2. After this, mix the cream with egg yolks and transfer in the Crock Pot.
3. Cook the mixture on low for 5 hours. Stir the liquid from time to time.
4. After this, mix the cream mixture with bananas and blend until smooth.
5. Place the mixture in the plastic vessel and refrigerate until solid.

Nutrition Info:
- Per Serving: 392 calories, 5.8g protein, 80.4g carbohydrates, 8.6g fat, 6.1g fiber, 221mg cholesterol, 30mg sodium, 885mg potassium.

Apple Compote

Servings: 2 | Cooking Time: 1 Hour

Ingredients:
- 1 pound apples, cored and cut into wedges
- ½ cup water
- 1 tablespoon sugar
- 1 teaspoon vanilla extract
- ½ teaspoon almond extract

Directions:
1. In your Crock Pot, mix the apples with the water and the other ingredients, toss, put the lid on and cook on High for 1 hour.
2. Divide into bowls and serve cold.

Nutrition Info:
- calories 203, fat 0, fiber 1, carbs 5, protein 4

Coconut And Macadamia Cream

Servings: 4 | Cooking Time: 1 Hour And 30 Minutes

Ingredients:
- 4 tablespoons vegetable oil
- 3 tablespoons macadamia nuts, chopped
- 2 tablespoons sugar
- 1 cup heavy cream
- 5 tablespoons coconut powder

Directions:
1. Put the oil in your Crock Pot, add nuts, sugar, coconut powder and cream, stir, cover, cook on Low for 1 hour and 30 minutes.
2. Stir well, divide into bowls and serve.

Nutrition Info:
- calories 154, fat 1, fiber 0, carbs 7, protein 2

Caramel Sauce Poached Pears

Servings: 6 | Cooking Time: 6 1/2 Hours

Ingredients:
- 6 ripe but firm pears, peeled and cored
- 1 1/2 cups caramel sauce
- 1 1/2 cups white wine
- 1 cinnamon stick
- 1 pinch salt

Directions:
1. Combine all the ingredients in your crock pot.
2. Cover the pot and cook on low settings for 6 hours.
3. Allow the pears to cool in the cooking liquid before serving.

Banana Chia Seeds Pudding

Servings:2 | Cooking Time: 5 Hours

Ingredients:
- 1 cup milk
- 4 tablespoons chia seeds
- 2 bananas, chopped

Directions:
1. Mix milk with chia seeds and pour in the Crock Pot.
2. Cook the liquid on Low for 5 hours.
3. Meanwhile, put the chopped bananas in the bottom of glass jars.
4. When the pudding is cooked, pour it over the bananas.

Nutrition Info:

- Per Serving: 304 calories, 10g protein, 44.9g carbohydrates, 11.6g fat, 12.8g fiber, 10mg cholesterol, 63mg sodium, 608mg potassium.

Glazed Bacon

Servings:4 | Cooking Time: 2 Hours

Ingredients:
- 4 bacon slices
- 1 tablespoon butter
- 3 tablespoons water
- 5 tablespoons maple syrup

Directions:
1. Put all ingredients in the Crock Pot.
2. Close the lid and cook the dessert on High for 2 hours.
3. Then transfer the bacon in the serving plates and top with maple syrup mixture from the Crock Pot.

Nutrition Info:
- Per Serving: 193 calories, 7.1g protein, 17g carbohydrates, 10.9g fat, 0g fiber, 29mg cholesterol, 462mg sodium, 159mg potassium.

Ricotta Bake With Dates And Nuts

Servings:3 | Cooking Time: 2.5 Hours

Ingredients:
- 2 oz nuts, chopped
- 2 dates, chopped
- 1 cup ricotta cheese
- 2 tablespoons of liquid honey
- 1 egg, beaten

Directions:
1. Mix ricotta cheese with buts and eggs and transfer in the ramekins.
2. Put the ramekins in the Crock Pot and close the lid.
3. Cook the dessert on High for 2.5 hours.
4. Then top the ramekins with dates and liquid honey.

Nutrition Info:
- Per Serving: 305 calories, 14.7g protein, 24.8g carbohydrates, 17.7g fat, 2.2g fiber, 80mg cholesterol, 251mg sodium, 279mg potassium.

Amaranth Bars

Servings:7 | Cooking Time: 1 Hour

Ingredients:
- ½ cup amaranth
- 4 oz peanuts, chopped
- ¼ cup of coconut oil
- 3 oz milk chocolate, chopped

Directions:
1. Put all ingredients in the Crock Pot and cook on High for 1 hour.
2. Then transfer the melted amaranth mixture in the silicone mold, flatten it, and refrigerate until solid.
3. Cut the dessert into bars.

Nutrition Info:
- Per Serving: 276 calories, 7.1g protein, 19.1g carbohydrates, 20.3g fat, 3.1g fiber, 3mg cholesterol, 15mg sodium, 210mg potassium.

Coconut And Mango Mousse

Servings:3 | Cooking Time: 7 Hours

Ingredients:
- 1 cup coconut cream
- 3 egg yolks
- 3 tablespoons sugar
- 1 teaspoon vanilla extract
- 1 mango, peeled, chopped, pureed

Directions:
1. Mix egg yolks with sugar and blend until smooth.
2. Pour the liquid in the Crock Pot, add coconut cream, and stir carefully.
3. Close the lid and cook it on Low for 7 hours.
4. After this, stir the mixture well and pour in the glasses.
5. Add mango puree.

Nutrition Info:
- Per Serving: 354 calories, 5.5g protein, 34g carbohydrates, 24g fat, 3.6g fiber, 210mg cholesterol, 21mg sodium, 419mg potassium.

Blueberry Tapioca Pudding

Servings:4 | Cooking Time: 3 Hours

Ingredients:
- 4 teaspoons blueberry jam
- 4 tablespoons tapioca
- 2 cups of milk

Directions:
1. Mix tapioca with milk and pour it in the Crock Pot.
2. Close the lid and cook the liquid on low for 3 hours.
3. Then put the blueberry jam in 4 ramekins.
4. Cool the cooked tapioca pudding until warm and pour over the jam.

Nutrition Info:
- Per Serving: 112 calories, 4.1g protein, 18.8g carbohydrates, 2.5g fat, 0.1g fiber, 10mg cholesterol, 58mg sodium, 71mg potassium.

Baked Camembert

Servings:6 | Cooking Time: 1.5 Hours

Ingredients:
- 1-pound camembert
- 1 oz walnuts, chopped
- 2 tablespoons of liquid honey

Directions:
1. Line the Crock Pot with baking paper.
2. Then put the camembert in the bottom of the Crock Pot and close the lid.
3. Cook the meal on High for 1.5 hours.
4. Then make the circle in the camembert with the help of the knife.
5. Sprinkle the cooked cheese with liquid honey and walnuts.

Nutrition Info:
- Per Serving: 277 calories, 16.1g protein, 6.6g carbohydrates, 21.1g fat, 0.3g fiber, 54mg cholesterol, 637mg sodium, 170mg potassium.

Caramel

Servings:10 | Cooking Time: 7 Hours

Ingredients:
- 1 cup of sugar
- 1 cup heavy cream
- 2 tablespoons butter

Directions:
1. Put sugar in the Crock Pot.
2. Add heavy cream and butter.
3. Close the lid and cook the caramel on Low for 7 hours.
4. Carefully mix the cooked caramel and transfer it in the glass cans.

Nutrition Info:
- Per Serving: 137 calories, 0.3g protein, 20.3g carbohydrates, 6.7g fat, 0g fiber,23mg cholesterol, 21mg sodium, 10mg potassium.

APPENDIX : Recipes Index

C

Made in the USA
Middletown, DE
17 March 2023

26936717R00077